Sexual Harassment
and
Sexual Abuse

Sexual Harassment and Sexual Abuse

A Handbook for Teachers and Administrators

Audrey Cohan
Mary Ann Hergenrother
Yolanda M. Johnson
Laurie S. Mandel
Janice Sawyer

CORWIN PRESS, INC.
A Sage Publications Company
Thousand Oaks, California

For information address:

Corwin Press, Inc.
A Sage Publications Company
2455 Teller Road
Thousand Oaks, California 91320
e-mail: order@corwin.sagepub.com

SAGE Publications Ltd.
6 Bonhill Street
London EC2A 4PU
United Kingdom

SAGE Publications India Pvt. Ltd.
M-32 Market
Greater Kailash I
New Delhi 110 048 India

Printed in the United States of America

Library of Congress Cataloging-in-Publication Data

Sexual harassment and sexual abuse : a handbook for teachers and
   administrators / Audrey Cohan . . . [et al.].
      p. cm.
   Includes bibliographical references (pp. 91-99).
   ISBN 0-8039-6440-4 (alk. paper). — ISBN 0-8039-6441-2 (pbk.: alk. paper)
      1. Sex harassment in education—United States—Handbooks, manuals,
   etc. 2. Child sexual abuse—United States—Handbooks, manuals, etc.
   3. Education and state—United States—Handbooks, manuals, etc.
   I. Cohan, Audrey.
   LC212.82.S498   1996
   370.19′345—dc20
                                                                    96-11128

This book is printed on acid-free paper.

96 97 98 99 00 10 9 8 7 6 5 4 3 2 1

Corwin Press Production Editor: S. Marlene Head

Contents

Preface   vii

Acknowledgments   viii

About the Authors   ix

Introduction   1

1. Defining Sexual Harassment and Abuse   3

   Review of the Literature   3
   Highlights of Research on Sexual Harassment
   and Sexual Abuse   10
   Laws and Litigation   16

2. Step-by-Step Procedures on How to Handle
   a Complaint   21

   Part 1: Sexual Abuse by a Staff Member   21
   Part 2: Sexual Harassment by a Peer or Adult   31
   Procedures for Investigating Sexual Harassment Complaints 37

3. Preventing Sexual Harassment and Abuse   57

   Part 1: Building a Safe Environment   57
   Part 2: Educating the Whole School Community   60
   Summary   74

Resource A: Videotapes   77

Resource B: Other Media   80

Resource C: Organizations   83

Resource D: Annotated Bibliography   85

Overview of Sexual Harassment   85
Curriculum Resources   86
Resources for Students   88
Comprehensive Resources for Districts   90

References and Suggested Readings   91

References   91
Suggested Readings   94

Preface

Deep concern for the safe passage of children through our schools leads us to try to resolve issues of sexual harassment and sexual abuse. We have studied the research and offer suggestions for handling allegations of sexual harassment or abuse should they arise in your school.

Although we have not solved the "whys" of sexual harassment and child sexual abuse, we can document an increase in the number of cases reported by students in recent years. Encouraged by students, as well as school staff, who have indicated that they want to change their schools, we have highlighted some ideas needed to promote change.

Our goal is to have parents, faculty, administrators, and staff take a closer look at their students' school lives and initiate change whenever possible. Ultimately, our hope is that the best educational experience, free of sexual harassment or child sexual abuse, will be provided for all students as they proceed through their school years.

Acknowledgments

We would like to thank Charol Shakeshaft, our mentor, who sparked our interest in issues of abuse and harassment and who offered encouragement, both professionally and personally. The idea of presenting our work in the form of a book came from Alice Foster who, with the help of Marlene Head, provided continuous guidance for writing and editing.

Ron Friedman shared his experiences and offered valuable feedback as well as his time. We gratefully acknowledge Lorna Lewis, Edward Stancik, and Bart Zabin for sharing their insight into the problems surrounding sexual abuse and sexual harassment.

As always, our greatest personal support came from our families and friends.

AUDREY COHAN
Molloy College

MARY ANN HERGENROTHER
Cooperative Educational Services
Trumbull, CT

YOLANDA M. JOHNSON
LAURIE S. MANDEL
JANICE SAWYER
Hofstra University

About the Authors

Audrey Cohan, Ed.D., is an Assistant Professor of Education at Molloy College in New York. She is a graduate of the doctoral program at Hofstra University, where she began her research on the sexual abuse of children within schools.

Mary Ann Hergenrother is the program administrator for a regional special education program for students with behavioral and emotional problems that is sponsored by Cooperative Educational Services of Trumbull, CT. She also serves as a consultant to schools on issues of gender equity, diversity, and special education.

Yolanda M. Johnson is an adjunct instructor and research assistant at Hofstra University. She also serves as an educational consultant for program development. Her research interests include parenting and families as educators.

Laurie S. Mandel is a research assistant and doctoral candidate in the Department of Administration and Policy Studies and an adjunct instructor in the School of Education at Hofstra University. Her dissertation research explores how gender and sexuality norms shape adolescent gender identity

Janice Sawyer, Ed.D., is an adjunct Assistant Professor in the School of Education at Hofstra University. Her research interests include school climate and peer interactions. She also serves as a consultant

to schools on issues of peer sexual harassment in the areas of student
and staff training and curriculum development.

Introduction

In 1989, as part of a larger study led by Dr. Charol Shakeshaft, Audrey Cohan began examining incidents of sexual abuse of students by teachers and administrators. The highly controversial case at that time was the McMartin trial in California, in which it was alleged that preschoolers had been sexually abused. At the time, many thought that the sexual abuse of children in a school setting was a new phenomenon. It appears, however, that sexual abuse and its long-term effects had simply begun to make their way into society's consciousness.

In 1993, with the publication of the AAUW Survey of Sexual Harassment in Schools, the focus began to shift, and the definitions of abuse and harassment seemed to overlap. As members of a research team led by Dr. Charol Shakeshaft, the following individuals began researching peer harassment in schools: Mary Ann Hergenrother, Yolanda M. Johnson, Laurie S. Mandel, and Janice Sawyer.

In this handbook, we will examine issues of sexual abuse when perpetrated by adult staff members. We will also address issues of sexual harassment, focusing on both adult-to-student and student-to-student interactions. We hope this book will guide educators in resolving issues of sexual harassment and sexual abuse that are certain to come up in schools.

The purpose of this handbook, therefore, is to define sexual harassment and sexual abuse in schools, help others recognize sexual harassment and abuse, suggest ways to create and foster an environment that will be healthy and free of harassment and abuse, outline the best way to handle complaints, and propose policies and procedures that will be supportive to both staff and students.

1

1

Defining Sexual
Harassment and Abuse

Review of the Literature

It seems that at least weekly we can pick up a magazine or a newspaper or listen to a news broadcast of an incident of sexual harassment or sexual abuse. In recent years, an increasing number of incidents have occurred in schools. It is no longer uncommon to hear about a teacher sexually abusing a student, or a student harassing a peer so that the child is afraid to go to school. Ironically and sadly, many of these incidents happen in schools, the places parents send their children and where they expect them to be both cared for and safe.

As an administrator, ask yourself these five questions about your school:

1. Do students comment to other students about the way their bodies look?
2. Are students "rating" other students on their physical appearance as they walk through the halls?
3. Do teachers grab, touch, or pinch students in a friendly way?
4. Are students or teachers displaying or circulating sexually explicit materials?
5. Are students whistling or making cat calls in the hallways?

If any of the answers are yes, you need to know more. We will define sexual harassment and sexual abuse as they exist in schools as well as give an overview of current literature. Sexual harassment and sexual abuse have been defined many ways, often depending on the author or agency reporting the behavior. In the past several years, the terms *harassment* and *abuse* have been used synonymously. Here, we will try to differentiate between sexual harassment and child sexual abuse.

How do I know if the behavior by the teacher or staff member constitutes sexual abuse?

Sexual abuse is the exploitation of a student for the sexual gratification of a staff member, who is an adult. The relationship is always one of power because teachers are charged with the care, safety, and protection of children.

What is sexual harassment?

Under Title VII of the 1964 Civil Rights Act, sexual harassment in the workplace is a form of sex discrimination. In 1980, the federal government issued criteria to help assess whether "unwelcome" sexual advances, requests for sexual favors, or other verbal and physical conduct of a sexual nature constitute sexual harassment.

Unwelcome sexual advances, requests for sexual favors, and other verbal or physical conduct of a sexual nature constitute sexual harassment when:

1. Submission to such conduct is made either explicitly or implicitly a term or condition of a person's employment
2. Submission to or rejection of such conduct by an individual is used as the basis for decisions affecting an individual's employment
3. Such conduct has the purpose or effect of unreasonably interfering with a person's work (Equal Employment Opportunity Commission, Federal Register, November 10, 1980)

What is sexual harassment in a school setting?

The italicized wording added to the EEOC definition helps us to understand sexual harassment in an educational setting.

> Unwelcome sexual advances, requests for sexual favors, and other verbal or physical conduct of a sexual nature constitute sexual harassment when:
>
> 1. Submission to such conduct is made either explicitly or implicitly a term or condition of a person's employment or *academic advancement*
> 2. Submission to or rejection of such conduct by an individual is used as the basis for decisions affecting an individual's employment or *academic standing*
> 3. Such conduct has the purpose or effect of unreasonably interfering with a person's work or *academic performance*—or creating an intimidating, hostile or offensive work, *learning or social environment* (Resnick-Sandler & Paludi, 1993, pp. 25-26)

In educational settings, sexual harassment of students is a form of sex discrimination that violates Title IX of the Education Amendments of 1972. In 1981, the Office for Civil Rights of the U.S. Department of Education issued a policy memorandum generally defining sexual harassment that would violate Title IX in schools:

> Sexual harassment consists of verbal or physical conduct of a sexual nature, imposed on the basis of sex, by an employee or an agent of a recipient that denies, limits, provides different, or conditions the provisions of aid, benefits, services or treatment protected under Title IX. (Office for Civil Rights, U.S. Department of Education, August 31, 1981)

There are two types of sexual harassment:

Quid pro quo. Quid pro quo sexual harassment consists of something received or withheld in exchange for sexual favors, such as promotions or student grades. Examples:

1. A teacher offers an A to a student who will have sex with him or her.
2. A coach provides more playing opportunities for a student who has sex with him or her.
3. A student in student government may be in a position of authority that promises a benefit in exchange for sexual favors.

Although quid pro quo harassment may not be the most pervasive form of sexual harassment, it does violate Title IX requirements and may lead to further legal action. For an interaction or incident to be considered quid pro quo harassment, it need happen only once. Quid pro quo sexual harassment has the following major characteristics:

- It involves sexual demands or advances that are unwanted.
- Submission to or rejection of these advances is explicitly or implicitly a term or condition of educational school status, instruction, or participation in educational or extracurricular activities.
- Submission to or rejection of such conduct by a student is used as the basis for decisions about his or her school status or academic evaluation.

Hostile environment. Hostile environment sexual harassment occurs when a work or school environment is so offensive or hostile that it interferes with an individual's ability to work or with a student's ability to learn or to participate in learning activities in and around the school environment. Harassment that is sexual in nature may be verbal, visual, or physical.

Examples of hostile environment sexual harassment include the following:

1. A teacher repeatedly tells dirty jokes or makes sexist remarks.
2. Sexually explicit or suggestive graffiti is written on desks, lockers, or bathroom walls.
3. Males brag about the size of, or allude to, their penises.

Institutions that tolerate or allow such behaviors that can create a hostile environment can be held liable under Title IX for not stopping the harassing behaviors.

The U.S. Department of Education, which enforces Title IX, considers a hostile environment to be one that interferes with a student's ability to receive an equal opportunity education; hence it is discriminatory and a violation of Title IX. Yet hostile environment sexual harassment is far more prevalent than quid pro quo sexual harassment. However, hostile environment harassment is harder for some people to recognize and acknowledge because the harassing behaviors are frequently construed as "normal" developmental behaviors or rationalized as "boys will be boys." Again, sexual harassment is unwanted or unwelcome sexual or gender-based behavior by a person who has formal (such as teacher-to-student) or informal (such as student-to-student) power over another.

Any sexual behavior between adults and students in school is considered sexual abuse; the notion of "wanted or unwanted" does not apply in such cases.

Keep in mind that even in situations where the teacher and student may be close in age (as in the example of a 23-year-old teacher and a high school senior), the sexual behavior is still considered sexual abuse. It is sexual abuse by virtue of the teacher-student roles and is not dependent on the age of consent.

Forms of sexual harassment and sexual abuse. Sexual harassment and sexual abuse may take the form of verbal, visual, or physical abuse. It may involve the following relationships:

- Adult to student: This form of sexual harassment is illegal under Title IX and may carry criminal charges.
- Student to student: This form of sexual harassment in schools is illegal under Title IX.
- Adult to adult: This form of sexual harassment is illegal under Title VII.
- Student to adult: This form of sexual harassment is illegal under Title VII.

Recent legal decisions are helping education professionals clarify their understanding of peer sexual harassment and child sexual abuse in schools. School officials are hearing a resounding wake-up call from the courts that they have a duty to protect children from harm and violation of their basic civil rights. That the school has a legal and ethical responsibility to protect students from such harm has been underscored by a recent spate of court decisions (Heubert, 1994).

Based on recent empirical studies of student-to-student sexual harassment, we know that suggestive looks, comments, gestures, or jokes and unwanted touching or grabbing are the most common forms of peer harassment in the schools (American Association of University Women [AAUW], 1993; Stein, Marshall, & Tropp, 1993). Below are numerous examples of what is considered sexual harassment among students when the behavior or interaction is unwanted.

Examples of peer-to-peer sexual harassment are

- Teasing other students about body development, either overdevelopment or underdevelopment
- Calling girls "slut," "whore," "fat," "cow," or "lesbo," or calling boys "homo," "fag," or "queer." (Using homophobic words, such as *faggot, homo, queer,* and *sissy* also is a form of sexual harassment) (AAUW, 1993)
- Describing sexual fantasies
- Whistling or yelling obscenities at girls in school
- Threatening rape
- Teasing students about their sexual activities or their lack of sexual activity
- Calling another student gay or lesbian
- Girls yelling in the hallway that someone has a "hard on"
- Making sexist remarks or dirty jokes
- "Rating" other students on physical appearance/attributes
- "Cornering" a student in a sexual way
- Touching, grabbing, or pinching in a sexual way
- Forcing someone to kiss (male/female)
- Making sexual gestures; imitating masturbation or intercourse

- Boys grabbing their groins when girls pass by
- Students giving other students "the finger"
- Students displaying or circulating centerfolds or sexually explicit materials
- Passing sexually descriptive letters or notes
- Writing sexually descriptive or suggestive graffiti on classroom desks, chalkboards, bathroom walls, etc.
- Spreading sexual rumors

In addition to knowing the definitions and examples provided in this chapter, it is imperative that school policy makers have a thorough understanding of how students experience what may be considered sexual harassment or abuse—how it impacts on their lives in school and how education professionals can appropriately respond.

Effective school responses to student sexual harassment and sexual abuse include several important components. Sexual harassment or abuse as it applies to school employees or other students should be clearly defined in school policy. These policies, along with specific procedures for a swift and thorough investigation, should be systematically communicated to all school employees, to all parents and parent groups, and to students. Educational efforts to ensure that members of all groups have a thorough understanding of the problem, the steps the school will take to address it, and the consequences for violations should be ongoing and institutionalized. Educational programs appropriate for each group can be developed and implemented routinely, similar to the way schools address appropriate and inappropriate cafeteria and fire drill behavior. Definitions and examples of harassing or abusive social interactions and their impact on people can be integrated into the school's curriculum to stimulate ongoing discussion and promote increased awareness, sensitivity, and understanding among students.

In conclusion, schools need information that will enable them to address effectively sexual harassment and abuse by students or adults as it occurs. A better understanding of the prevalence and impact of peer sexual harassment or child sexual abuse on student behavior and performance will help educational professionals develop appropriate practices and policies that may assist them in their efforts to create a safe, healthy, and caring school environment.

Highlights of Research
on Sexual Harassment and Sexual Abuse

Sexual Harassment in Schools

Significant studies that examine the sexual harassment of students in schools include the 1993 AAUW study, "Hostile Hallways," and the 1993 *Seventeen* magazine study reported in "Secrets in Public: Sexual Harassment in Our Schools."

The AAUW (1993) report of a survey of more than 1,632 female and male public school students in Grades 8 through 12 from 79 school districts was representative of a diverse group of students. These students were asked to fill out a survey that included this question: "During your whole school life, how often, if at all, has anyone (this includes students, teachers, other school employees, and anyone else) done the following things to you *when you did not want them to?*" Students answered "often," "occasionally," "rarely," "never," and "not sure" in response to the following:

- Made sexual comments, jokes, or looks
- Showed, gave, or left you sexual pictures, photographs, illustrations, messages, or notes
- Wrote sexual messages or graffiti about you on bathroom walls, in locker rooms, etc.
- Spread sexual rumors about you
- Said you were gay or lesbian
- Spied on you as you dressed or showered at school
- Flashed or mooned you
- Touched, grabbed, or pinched you in a sexual way
- Pulled at your clothing in a sexual way
- Intentionally brushed against you in a sexual way
- Pulled your clothing off or down
- Blocked your way or cornered you in a sexual way
- Forced you to kiss him or her
- Forced you to do something sexual, other than kissing (AAUW, 1993)

The findings indicate that sexual harassment, both verbal and physical, is experienced on a daily basis by most students.

A second study that researched peer sexual harassment is the *Seventeen* magazine survey by Nan Stein, Nancy L. Marshall, and Linda R. Tropp (1993), which was a joint project of the NOW Legal Defense and Education Fund and the Wellesley College Center for Research on Women. Reported in "Secrets in Public: Sexual Harassment in Our Schools" were the results of a survey using two open-ended questions and a questionnaire composed of 13 questions. The open-ended questions asked girls to talk about what schools should be doing about harassment and, if they had been sexually harassed, how it made them feel.

More than 4,200 girls completed and returned surveys. Of these responses, 2,002 letters were randomly selected for analysis. Girls who completed the surveys were in Grades 2 through 12, and their ages ranged from 9 to 19 years. Most of the girls (90%) attended public schools. Six percent attended private nonparochial schools, 3% attended parochial schools, and just under 1% attended vocational schools. All but one of these institutions were coeducational. In addition, the girls came from a variety of racial and ethnic groups: 89% Caucasian, 2% African American, 3% Latina or Hispanic, 2% Asian American, 0.6% Native American, and 3% of mixed racial or ethnic backgrounds (Stein et al., 1993). The following findings emerged from the survey:

- The most common forms of sexual harassment are receiving comments, gestures, or looks and being touched, pinched, or grabbed.
- Most harassers are male.
- Girls are more likely to do nothing or to walk away (without telling the harasser to stop) if the harasser is a teacher, administrator, or other staff member than if the harasser is a fellow student.
- Schools are less likely to do something about a harassment incident when the harasser is a teacher.
- When girls told a teacher or administrator about the harassment, nothing happened to the harasser in 45% of the incidents reported.

- Only 8% of the girls reported that their schools had, and enforced, a policy on sexual harassment.
- When sexual harassment occurs, it is *not* a one-time-only event: 39% of the girls and young women reported being harassed at school on a daily basis during the past year.
- Harassment is a public event: Other people are present at more than two thirds of the incidents reported.
- Sexual harassment happens in all kinds of schools and to all kinds of girls—there are few differences by type of school attended or by racial or ethnic background.

In their discussion of the survey, the authors describe urgent notes scribbled on envelopes in which girls detailed incidents of harassment perpetrated by peers and sometimes by adults. In their letters, they wrote of anger and frustration directed at adults who refused to intervene. The girls in this study coded the adults' silences as negligence because they permitted the harassment to continue.

The students in this survey also were asked how the schools responded to the specific situation. The girls reported that in 85% of the cases, nothing happened to the harassers. In 15% of the cases, the harasser received a reprimand or warning, was suspended or expelled, or was dismissed or resigned (if a school employee) when the students told a teacher or school administrator.

Stein et al. (1993) found that when girls report abuse to administrators, their complaints are dismissed. In fact, the administrators frequently rationalize the boys' behavior as teasing or "boys being boys." The researchers also noted that adults did not believe the girls' stories. Furthermore, these accounts are not atypical. They are repeated every day in every community, from large urban settings to suburban areas to rural communities. If girls resist by yelling or hitting or telling harassers to stop, it is not enough to end the harassment.

With children ages 12 and older, harassment is all too often dismissed as "typical adolescent behavior" and misconstrued as a normal rite of passage or as awkward "getting-to-know-you" behaviors. It is trivialized, condoned, or described as "flirting" or "initiation rites" (Stein, 1991).

The "Secrets in Public" survey concludes that sexual harassment is rampant in high schools. More than 89% of the girls in the sample reported verbal abuse, and 83% of the sample reported physical abuse. In this study, 96% of the girls stated that they were harassed by male peers.

In the *Journal for a Just and Caring Education,* Shakeshaft et al. (1995) discuss how peers treat each other in ways that are less than supportive and helpful. Moreover, this study on peer interaction found that "school is a harassing and unkind place for most students" (p. 35). Some of the major observations made by Shakeshaft et al. include the following:

- Harassment is mostly verbal for both girls and boys.
- Girls are harassed for how they look, such as their body shapes or breast size.
- Boys are harassed for how they behave—whether they conform to a standard "male" model.
- Girls are called sluts, whores, and bitches.
- Boys are called faggots and queers.
- The worst insult for both is to be put into a role that is one of the female stereotypes.
- Students say they feel powerless and look to adults to intervene and stop the harassment.

Sexual Abuse in Schools

McEvoy (1990) cites the 1980s as a most prolific time in the expansion of child abuse laws, for in that decade, more than 400 pieces of abuse and neglect legislation were passed affecting schools and agencies. This legislative activity may have been sparked by the passage of the 1974 Federal Child Abuse Prevention and Treatment Act.

The National Committee for Prevention of Child Abuse (1989) recognizes sexual abuse as one of four categories of child abuse; the others are physical abuse, emotional abuse, and neglect. The sexual abuse component is "exploitation of a child for the sexual gratification of an adult, as in rape, incest, fondling of the genitals, exhibitionism, or pornography" (p. 4). Whatever the age of the perpetrator, if the target of these behaviors is a child, these activities constitute sexual abuse.

Legal definitions may vary from state to state, as do the common definitions used on a daily basis. A generally agreed-upon definition is that child sexual abuse is behavior that is sexual in nature, unwelcome, and in which the adult party holds some form of power or control over the minor party, as in a teacher-student relationship.

Bithell (1991) was one of the first researchers to try to quantify sexual abuse by teachers against students. She offered a definition of the "educator sexual abuse offender" as anyone who has sexually abused a child while having the child in his or her care in a school setting. She defined the "student victim" as any child under the age of 18 who has been sexually abused by an educator who has responsibility for the student in a school setting. We would add that the staff member need not have direct responsibility for the student, but may have access to the student through the school setting.

Conte (1986), in his work for the National Committee for Prevention of Child Abuse, has highlighted six features that may be helpful to consider when trying to determine if sexual abuse has occurred. One or more of these factors may be considered, and we have expanded on these factors to include school-related issues.

Lack of consent. Children cannot give consent for sexual contact with adults and therefore their participation does not indicate that consent has been given. Furthermore, when a child fails to report the abuse, this does not indicate that consent has been given. Very often, the silence of a child is viewed as a form of consent, which is not so. In school settings, children often do not feel that they have any say about a teacher's actions.

Ambivalence. With sexual abuse, there may be seemingly positive dimensions for victimized children. For instance, a child may receive special attention, rewards, or privileges while in the school setting. These situations may create ambivalence for the child who enjoys being the "teacher's pet" or who is pleased to receive good grades. A child may welcome being told that he or she is the teacher's favorite student; for example, a third-grade teacher who says, "I like you the best and that's why I want to help you the most."

Exploitation. Sexual abuse usually involves some form of exploitation in which the older person uses knowledge, skills, or resources to manipulate or coerce the child. For instance, a teacher may be privy to a child's personal problems or family difficulties and use this information to gain further control over the child.

Force. Conte has argued that in cases of sexual abuse, force is used. You need not only think of physical force; psychological force also can be used to gain access to children and keep their silence. In some cases, students have reported that fear of reprisals from their teachers kept them silent.

Intent. The intent of the behavior is important in deciding whether or not the behavior is abusive. If the intent is to satisfy the adult sexually, then the behavior is abusive. Sexual gratification for the adult is the key and helps to explain why the visual element of showing pornographic pictures to students makes the behavior sexually abusive.

Secrecy. There are a number of strategies that abusers will use to maintain silence about the relationship. Conte lists them as threat, force, bribery, intimidation, and physical or psychological coercion.

Berliner and Conte (1990) cite that both victims and offenders have described a grooming process that precedes sexual abuse. They refer to this as the "sexualization" of the relationship, or a gradual process designed to engage the child in sexual activity. Schools may be the perfect place for a slow, unnoticed process of sexualization to occur. Students see their teachers on a daily basis, often seek their support or counseling, and are encouraged to talk and interact with their teachers. Berliner and Conte outline several behaviors, such as hugging, massaging, snuggling, or wrestling, that may appear to be normal affectionate contact but can progressively become sexual acts.

The Federation on Child Abuse and Neglect (1992) developed a statement concerning the protection of children in school settings and asked that all local districts develop policies to deal with inappropriate or abusive behaviors on the part of school staff toward children. It states:

> Schools represent community islands of safety, where teachers and other personnel are vested with authority to guide children. As in all other areas where public trust is granted, there is potential for abuse of that trust, and appropriate safeguards must be mandated. Such safeguards would protect children from abuse and also protect adults from unwarranted or frivolous allegations. Criminal action is now the only recourse available where a school district fails to

respond to charges brought by parents or others concerned with the child's welfare. This is insufficient and fails to offer the protection expected. (p. 1)

This handbook is designed to guide educators and administrators in establishing policies that will protect students from sexual harassment and abuse and create safe and healthy schools.

Laws and Litigation

As Jay Heubert (1994) reflects,

The best way to deal with harassment is to prevent it, something educators are better equipped than lawyers or judges to do. But such efforts occur against the background of societal norms, which the law both reflects and shapes. (p. 2)

Many school districts have begun to question exactly what constitutes harassment in an educational setting (Lawton, 1993). Some school districts are examining their policies, practices, and procedures and how they create a school climate that may be hospitable or hostile to the students, whereas other districts and their administrators continue to assume a casual approach to inappropriate behavior in the schools (Stein, 1993).

Sexual harassment of students is a form of discrimination based on sex that is prohibited under Title IX of the Education Amendments of 1972. In 1979, the U.S. Supreme Court stipulated that not only the federal government but also individuals could initiate lawsuits under this federal statute. In *Franklin v. Gwinett County School District* (1992), the Supreme Court further expanded the victim's right to redress under Title IX claims to include monetary compensation. In this landmark case, a student, Christine Franklin, sued her school district because of sexual harassment and abuse by her economics teacher. Christine alleged that the teacher frequently called her out of class, discussed the intimate details of sexual relations between him and his wife, asked Christine about the affectionate behavior between her and her boyfriend, and even phoned her at home.

During this 15-month period, Christine also alleged that the teacher pressured her several times into having sex with him on school grounds. When Christine reported the abuse to her guidance counselor, the counselor took the matter to the principal. The principal phoned Christine's mother to report that she was telling stories about a teacher. School officials did not conduct a thorough and timely investigation of the claims against the teacher. Christine's mother believed her daughter and filed a complaint with the Office of Civil Rights, which determined that her daughter's civil rights had been violated under Title IX. The court held in favor of the student, finding that (a) a teacher's sexual harassment of a student is prohibitable sex discrimination, and (b) a public school district, as an agency receiving federal financial assistance, has an unquestionable duty to prevent sex discrimination under Title IX. Thus an educational institution may lose federal funding if it is found in violation of Title IX. Furthermore, the Court expanded Title IX liability to include monetary damages for the individual claimant. Both institutions and school officials may be liable for monetary damages.

In 1991, the Minnesota Department of Human Rights awarded the first monetary compensation, $15,000, to a student, Katy Lyle, who was allegedly sexually harassed by peers in her Duluth, Minnesota, high school. Although this incident occurred prior to the Supreme Court's decision in *Franklin*, the State of Minnesota had already enacted a law prohibiting sexual harassment in schools. Katy Lyle sued under this statute. She alleged that she had suffered persistent emotional distress because of offensive graffiti about her that was of a sexual nature. The sexually explicit graffiti, such as "Katy Lyle is a whore," had been written about her on the boys' bathroom wall. Although Katy and her parents had complained to school officials 16 times, the graffiti remained on the walls for 18 months. Following this lawsuit, the district established school policies prohibiting peer sexual harassment and developed clear procedures for addressing the issue. Custodians, for example, now check for and remove graffiti daily (Natale, 1993).

During the past 5 years, the courts, along with state and federal agencies, have received increasing numbers of claims by students that they have been subjected to sexual harassment by other students or by school employees. In 1993, the Office for Civil Rights of the U.S.

Department of Education received 42 complaints of sexual harassment in elementary and secondary schools during the first 8 months of the fiscal year; in 1988, it received only 10 for the entire year (Natale, 1993). In the case of *Doe v. Petaluma City School District* (1993), a former junior high school student filed a $1 million lawsuit in federal court against her school district. During her 7th- and 8th-grade years, she was allegedly verbally harassed by peers about "having a hot dog in her pants," called names of a sexual nature (e.g., "slut," "hoe," and "hot dog bitch"), and also physically threatened and assaulted. Although Jane Doe and her parents repeatedly requested that school employees stop the harassment, insufficient action was taken by school officials to eliminate the abuse. This landmark case is still pending.

In 1993, the American Association of University Women sponsored the first nationwide survey ever conducted on harassment in the schools. It found that 86% of girls and 75% of boys reported experiencing sexual harassment while attending public school (AAUW, 1993). The AAUW concluded the following:

> Beyond a doubt, we now know that sexual harassment in the classrooms and hallways of America's schools is a major problem—one we can no longer afford to ignore. Unchecked, it will continue to deny millions of children the educational environment they need to grow into healthy, educated adults. (p. 2)

Eliminating sexual harassment in our schools is a nationwide concern. At the same time, many states, communities, and school districts are struggling to increase their ability to recognize and interrupt harassing behaviors that may interfere with a student's right to an education free from discrimination and hostility. As Adria Steinberg (1993) points out,

> It is easy to blame peer pressure and youth culture for everything from slipping grades to gang violence. It is harder to figure out how schools might create a positive social milieu for students. The status quo oozes with contradictions. (p. 1)

A growing number of states have already enacted laws prohibiting all forms of sexual harassment in elementary and secondary schools.

School districts are developing policies, procedures, and practices that may assist them in addressing effectively the problem of sexual harassment of and by students as it occurs.

2

Step-by-Step Procedures on How to Handle a Complaint

Part 1: Sexual Abuse by a Staff Member

What types of sexually abusive behaviors are likely to be reported by students when perpetrated by teachers?

- Viewing of pornographic materials
- Being called names that have a sexual innuendo
- Being asked about sexual activity
- 3eing touched on the back, breasts, or buttocks
- Being touched in the genital area
- Having intercourse

How to Handle a Student's Complaint

AS A TEACHER

Suppose a student comes to your classroom one morning and confides to you that a teacher in your school has touched him or her in an inappropriate way. The student states that he or she feels uncomfortable and does not wish to go to that class.

Teachers are required by law to be mandated reporters. It is not up to them to decide whether a student is telling the truth, exaggerating, embellishing, or lying. Although the mandatory reporting process may vary from state to state, the reporting law defines mandated reporters as those individuals in both public and private schools who *must* report any reasonable suspicion that a child is being abused. There are penalties for failure to report, which in some states may include civil liabilities. Mandated reporters include teachers, coaches, school officials, day care center workers, child care workers, psychologists, guidance counselors, employees or volunteers in residential facilities, and social workers.

As a teacher, look to the *school's* policy to determine to whom you should "report." Most schools have a liaison to handle reports. This individual may or may not be a school administrator. If a school policy is not in place or is unclear, report to the principal.

As a Building Principal or Administrator

Suppose a teacher comes to you and states that he or she has reason to suspect that a child has been sexually abused by a staff member in the school.

As a building principal or administrator, you should follow the specific procedures outlined in your school policy on sexual abuse. The following procedures are recommended for inclusion in any district policy on sexual abuse for school settings:

1. Notify the superintendent about the allegation. No one should interview the student before the superintendent takes charge of the case.
2. In the event of allegations, or even rumors, immediately contact parents or guardians of the children involved. We suggest that the child not be questioned, even briefly, in a formal or informal manner before contact is made with the parents or guardians.
3. Remember that confidentiality of the allegations, as well as the people involved, should be of primary importance.
4. Investigations should be handled by professionals and supervised by the superintendent.
5. Document everything pertinent to the case.

AS A SUPERINTENDENT

The Federation on Child Abuse and Neglect (1992) suggests that (a) responsibility for conducting investigations of reports of child abuse (not limited to child sexual abuse) in educational settings should be carried out by a special unit of highly trained people within the State Education Department and (b) time frames need to be established that would call for investigations to be commenced within 24 hours of the receipt of reports and for investigations to be completed within 60 days, with corrective action initiated by the school thereafter.

When a complaint of child abuse is made, the superintendent should

- Take complete charge of the case.
- Notify the parents or guardians of the students involved.
- Inform the school board of the allegations made.
- Notify the school attorney.
- Inform the teacher of the allegations made (without detail and in the simplest of terms) and temporarily reassign the teacher or staff member so that he or she has no contact with students. If necessary, and with notification to the school board, suspend the teacher with pay until the allegations can be confirmed or disproved.
- Document every event, discussion, conversation, or letter regarding the case.
- Conduct a diligent investigation or supervise a trained professional who will conduct the investigation. We recommend that trained and experienced professionals conduct the interviews. Local law enforcement experts may need to be notified depending on the individual case.
- Offer feedback to the victim so that he or she understands that the allegations were taken seriously and that follow-up procedures are being followed.
- If necessary, have a meeting with the staff and parents to outline the allegations and the procedures being followed. Otherwise, your district will be flooded with phone calls

and rumors. Do not be surprised if the community sup-
ports the staff member and reacts negatively toward the
student.

- Be ready to speak with reporters from both the newspaper
  and television, and have a prepared statement approved by
  the school attorney.
- Examine issues of liability with the district's attorney, because districts may be held legally responsible for action
  taken or inaction.

The superintendent should *not*

- Get caught in a web of secrecy that unfairly protects the
  teacher.
- Revictimize the teacher or student by having them inter-
  viewed more than one time.
- Encourage, ask, or demand that the staff member resign.

Superintendents also should take the following steps:

- Review school practices that may put students at risk, such
  as door-to-door fundraising activities.
- Keep abreast of changing law. In response to New Jersey's
  "Megan's Law," some states require that local communities
  be notified when sex offenders are paroled in their areas. If
  the procedure is for the school district to receive the information and then notify the community, design an action
  plan. One of the questions that has been raised is, Does a
  release of such information violate the offender's constitu-
  tional right to privacy? School districts are now involved in
  creating policy and deciding whether or not, or how to,
  release information about sex offenders into the school
  community.
- When hiring new teachers, do a thorough background check.
  Look for state personnel registers that report resignations or
  dismissals because of misconduct. State directors of certification can share with district superintendents information
  obtained from the National Association of State Directors

of Teacher Education and Certification (NASDTEC). This organization has developed a national clearinghouse from which state directors receive monthly updates listing certificates that have been invalidated.

- Look for gaps in resumés or job histories, or recommendations that are worded in a noncommittal way or that invite the hiring district to call for further information about a candidate. Call listed references and verify resumés. When hiring support staff, the application needs to be specific and thorough (e.g., hiring of paraprofessionals, teacher assistants, cafeteria workers, clerical staff, nurses, custodians, maintenance mechanics, and coaches or substitutes for any of these positions). Employees who are support staff are not licensed by the state. A Sample Reference Form is shown on page 25.

- Use all background checks that are available. Graves (1994) explains that some states have or are adopting laws that give them authority to fingerprint teachers and other school employees.

- If your school has community service requirements, be sure to check out each site. Students need to have field supervisors as well as an on-site supervisor.

- Screen all volunteers who work with the students in your district. Many districts encourage volunteers to patrol schoolyards or help children improve their reading skills. However, some individuals may volunteer simply to work with children for their own sexual gratification.

Procedures for Handling Child Sexual Abuse Complaints

Every district should have procedures in place for handling child sexual abuse. One individual from the school district should be selected to be in charge. This role can be filled by the superintendent, but need not always be. Often, the person in charge is an assistant superintendent, director, or supervisor.

The responsibility of this person (referred to here as the superintendent) is to oversee the entire procedure. A crisis team should be established at the onset. Often, such a team consists of the school

Sample Reference Form

Give the names of three references who have closely observed your work as an employee or student. Recommendations by present and former supervisors, principals and others are preferred.

Please print	1	2	3
Name			
Address			
(Include Zip Code)			
Telephone	( )	( )	( )

I hereby certify that the facts set forth in this application are true and complete to the best of my knowledge. I further acknowledge that any falsification or omission will be sufficient cause for disqualification or dismissal if employed, regardless of when discovered. I understand that investigative background inquiries may be made on myself including consumer credit, criminal convictions, motor vehicle, and other reports. These reports will include information as to my character, work habits, performance, and experience along with reasons for termination of past employment. Further, I understand that you will be requesting information from various Federal, State and other agencies which maintain records concerning my past activities related to my driving, credit, criminal, civil, and other experiences. I authorize, without reservation, any party or agency contacted by this employer to furnish the above-mentioned information and I waive any right of access to any such information. I hereby consent to your obtaining any of the information noted above.

Dated _____ 19___ Signature of Applicant_____

Developed by Elwood Public Schools, Greenlawn, New York.

psychologist, the school social worker, and the superintendent. Be sure to have a male representative to interview male students and a female representative to interview female students. The procedures should be broken up into three steps: report, investigate, and document.

REPORT

A simple incident report should be available in each school in the event of an allegation. Reports should fit on one page and appear user friendly. Too many specific questions or detailed questions may cause the student, parent, or staff member to abandon the report. The student, parent, or staff member should not in any way be encouraged to abandon a report. A Sample Report is shown on page 27.

INVESTIGATE

Investigations can be conducted by the superintendent or a trained professional, and this depends on the type of allegation. No action by a district administrator should interfere with the legal aspect of the allegation.

The following are common reasons that sexual abuse cases are not investigated properly.

- The educational community is not trained to recognize sexual abuse.
- The educational community is not trained in how to properly handle an investigation and conduct interviews about sexual abuse.
- Investigations are started before parents are notified.
- Reporting procedures are not clearly stated for educators, students, or parents.

DOCUMENT

The interviewer should document the events, and copies should be given to the superintendent. Hold all documents in strict confidence.

Sample Report

Date:

What happened:

When it happened:

Where it happened:

Who committed the offensive behavior:

Witness(es), if any:

What offender said/did:

What complainant said/did:

How complainant felt:

How offender responded:

Quotes:

Date: _____

Name and title of the person filing the report: _____

_____

Signature: _____

Commonly Asked Questions

1. What if there have been previous allegations? A common concern for superintendents during investigations is past allegations that suddenly come to light and of which they had no prior knowledge. Therefore, as soon as allegations are made, files and documents should be examined to see if there have been any previously reported cases. One reason past allegations may have been overlooked is that the school climate of past years did not encourage reporting to the highest level of school administration. Years ago, allegations often were handled at a lower level in the school organization, or charges were easily dismissed as being frivolous or unfounded. In recent years, however, there has been increased pressure on schools to report all cases of suspected child sexual abuse. This fact is of special significance for superintendents who, during an investigation, find a pattern of unreported or unsubstantiated complaints about a staff member.

2. What if the student doesn't make an allegation him- or herself? Regardless of how an allegation is made, it must be followed up. Possibly, the parents or friends may bring the allegation to light. It is the responsibility of the superintendent, upon learning of or having reason to suspect that an incident of sexual abuse has occurred, to begin an investigation. In this case, the superintendent should fill out the report and continue with Steps 2 and 3: investigate and document.

3. Should anonymous or indirect allegations be followed up? Absolutely. A sexually abused student is often experiencing low self-esteem and ambivalence. For instance, in situations where sexual abuse is occurring, the child may enjoy being the "teacher's pet" or be pleased to receive good grades. A third grader who is being sexually abused probably doesn't have the skills to write a formal complaint. A picture drawn by the child depicting the abuse may be the first clue.

The abuser may also be intimidating or coercing the child to keep the "secret." As a leader in the district, the superintendent must take seriously every allegation, signed or unsigned.

4. Is it sexual abuse if the student is giving consent? As we emphasized earlier in the book, children cannot give consent for sexual conduct, and therefore, participation does not indicate that consent has been given.

5. Why can't Child Protective Services handle the allegation? If there is abuse by a family member, or a nonfamily member who is not a school employee, then Child Protective Services should be contacted. However, cases that occur in the school building, off the school grounds, in the school bus, or on school property and are perpetrated by school personnel must be supervised by someone in the district. Law enforcement experts, attorneys, and child protection consultants may also have a role in the investigation, but such involvement does not absolve school authorities from their responsibility to conduct a thorough, independent investigation.

6. After the sexual abuse is stopped and the case is brought to resolution, what is the superintendent's role? The question will always remain: What are the consequences for the student-victim who has been sexually abused? The extent of the impact will vary with each individual. The literature on the long-term impact on victims of sexual abuse suggests that the lifetime effects for a child who has been abused by someone in a trusted role cannot be predicted. However, we do know that students who have been sexually abused appear to function differently from their nonabused counterparts. The eight behavioral factors cited by Conte and Schuerman (1988) are poor self-esteem, aggressive behavior, fearful behavior, overly conscientious behavior, concentration problems, withdrawal behavior, acting out, and anxious-to-please behavior.

Therefore, it is critical that appropriate counseling begin. This may mean that the district needs to provide counseling by an experienced professional who specializes in treating survivors of sexual abuse. Counseling can be provided by the school counselor if, in fact, he or she is trained in sexual abuse therapy. Keep in mind that when charges are brought and the family learns of the abuse, the family will most likely be in crisis and may not have the skills to cope with the allegations.

7. What should be done if the allegation appears to be false? If an allegation appears to be false, documentation should still be completed. Questions need to be asked as to why the allegation was made, and counseling may need to be provided.

8. Can a district be held responsible if a student has already graduated? Yes! An investigation is necessary as long as the staff member is still employed in your district.

9. What if a staff member sexually abuses a nondistrict student off the school grounds? Local statutes must be examined. Generally, employee discipline should be pursued even though the minor student does not go to the same school in which the staff member is employed. Staff members in schools are generally held to a higher standard of conduct by courts than is applied to adults in general because of their positions as role models.

10. What is the role of the school board concerning child sexual abuse cases? The primary role of the board is to adopt such policy or policies as are necessary and appropriate to provide evidence and direction to the entire school community relative to the issue of sexual harassment and abuse in the schools.

The role of the school board, consistent with local, state, and federal law, should be to openly condemn all sexually abusive behaviors by staff members. In the event that allegations are made against a staff member, the school board should be notified immediately and kept apprised of the investigation. The school board will be able to decide during the resolution phase if further legal action needs to be taken or if new disciplinary measures need to be enacted.

Part 2: Sexual Harassment by a Peer or Adult

What types of sexually harassing behaviors are likely to be reported by students?

- Touching inappropriately
- Pinching or grabbing breasts, buttocks, or genital area
- Threatening rape
- Spreading rumors about sexual activity or intercourse
- Graffiti seen on desks, bathroom walls, textbooks, and so on
- Sexual comments about penis size, breast size, and so on

Types of inappropriate touching or sexual comments vary depending on the students' grade level. The slang of elementary students regarding sexual acts varies somewhat from that used by middle and high school students.

Unfortunately, many scenes in advertisements or on television depict inappropriate touching or language. Educators and parents should clearly convey the message that such unwanted acts are illegal and harassing.

Differentiating Between Sexual Harassment and Flirting

Whether or not an act is sexual harassment is often unclear, not only for students but also for adults in school. It is not uncommon to hear a comment such as "Oh . . . he's just flirting, that means he likes you." Being liked is generally a good feeling; being made uncomfortable is not. Flirting can feel good, sexual harassment does not. Teachers and administrators sometimes do little to enable students—girls in particular—to develop a sense of empowerment and autonomy. It is particularly difficult for middle school or junior high school students to be able to distinguish appropriate from inappropriate interactions because of their own exploration of sexuality and relationships. Students and adults alike need to learn a "new" language to be able to identify for themselves what is appropriate and inappropriate. Teaching students this new language will empower them by distinguishing and naming feelings that feel good, welcome, and fun from feelings that feel bad, unwelcome, or humiliating. The following list, outlined in the *Educator's Guide to Controlling Sexual Harassment* (Resnick-Sandler & Paludi, 1994), distinguishes between two very different sets of feelings—one evoked by flirting and the other by sexual harassment.

Flirting	Sexual Harassment
• Feels good	• Feels bad
• Is reciprocal	• Is one-sided
• Makes you feel attractive	• Makes you feel unattractive
• Is a compliment	• Is degrading
• Keeps you in control	• Makes you feel powerless
• Is equality based	• Is power based
• Involves positive touching	• Involves negative touching
• Is wanted	• Is unwanted
• Is legal	• Is illegal
• Is open	• Is invading
• Is flattering	• Is demeaning
• Makes you happy	• Makes you feel sad or angry
• Fosters positive self-esteem	• Fosters negative self-esteem

Roots of Sexual Harassment

For many years, gender equity researchers have documented evidence of the pervasiveness of gender-role stereotyping and bias within student-teacher interactions, curriculum materials, classroom behaviors, and course offerings. Only recently has sexual harassment caught the attention of these researchers.

From birth, children are taught the norms, values, and behaviors of their gender in their culture—what it means to be a girl or a boy. Through socialization, children internalize the rules for "masculinity" and "femininity," or what is appropriate behavior for females and males. Sexual harassment is largely a result of how girls and boys are socialized, that is, the kinds of messages that girls and boys receive about how they are supposed to act because of their gender.

As girls and boys move into middle and junior high school, a time that is highly sexualized for adolescents, they act out their behaviors and attitudes about females and males through language and actions. Attitudes toward girls as well as "nonmasculine" boys that are disrespectful, denigrating, and sexually harassing are all too common.

Sexual harassment, at best an act of disrespect and at worst a strand of violence in our culture, is based in part on cultural assumptions about "appropriate" gender roles for males and females. Boys in our culture are generally socialized to be aggressive, powerful, unemotional, and controlling, whereas girls in our culture are largely socialized to be dependent and less aggressive. Although gender roles are changing, it is these norms that are still deeply rooted gender-role stereotypes in our society. The expectation and permission given to boys for acting aggressively contributes to disrespect and violence against girls and women. Boys are still encouraged to be very masculine by attitudes such as "boys will be boys," "fight like a man," or "boys don't cry." If they violate these norms, they often are teased for being a "sissy" or a "wimp." This is a form of sexual harassment. Stereotyped perceptions of what it means to be appropriately masculine and appropriately feminine are glorified in the media and reinforced in our schools. We also see this in our schools—in textbooks, children's books, and interactions among peers and in classrooms.

Sexual harassment is a way in which boys demonstrate their masculinity in their relations with girls, women, and other boys. Although not all boys are violent, most incidents of sexual harassment are committed by boys and directed at girls; such behaviors have rarely been censured because they have been considered expressions of normal, healthy masculinity. Among adolescents, this is evident in the disrespectful ways in which boys insult, tease, and degrade girls and other boys without regard for how and why their behaviors negatively affect others and can be considered sexual harassment. By and large, schools have not yet developed environments that provide young men with adequate emotional and intellectual support. Instead, developing a strong, macho masculinity continues to be the norm for boys. "One of the ways in which boys learn about and practice their masculine behavior—including sexual harassment—is in interactions with others in schools" (Halson, 1989, p. 137). Likewise, girls usually ignore or do not code boys' behaviors as sexual harassment, and they accept the inevitability of it because they typically are not taught to challenge boys' behaviors. "It is as if there is a war going on and the girls have no ammunition with which to respond to the violence they suffer" (Halson, 1989, p. 139).

Sexual harassment is a form of violence commonly experienced by young women, and schools sanction it through nonintervention. Thus schools often help to reproduce, rather than challenge, existing imbalances of power between males and females (Halson, 1989). Remember, sexual harassment is about power, and power imbalances exist where inequity exists. As long as girls and boys are not viewed and treated as equals, sexual harassment cannot be eradicated from our culture and from our schools. Schools that commit to gender equity thus commit to changing the balance of power between girls and boys in various ways. These schools have the greatest chance of minimizing the extent to which young women and young men are subjected to sexual harassment and the extent to which these experiences significantly affect their lives and personalities. Most important, perhaps, is that male and female attitudes toward each other need to be bridged by respect.

Schools are one of the most important systems for acculturating children to society, and our current school structure accepts violence and aggression as a male norm. It can be speculated that patterns of behaviors and attitudes about girls and boys that emerge in early elementary years and peak during adolescence may develop into domestic violence and sexual abuse in adult years. We must change to a paradigm that assumes male and female norms of empathy, compassion, and respect. Schools are key to this intervention in the socialization of girls and boys and in creating a harassment-free and gender-fair environment.

How to Handle a Student's Complaint

As a Teacher

Suppose a student comes to you one morning and states that he or she is being sexually harassed by another student. The student appears upset and states that his or her schoolwork is suffering, and that he or she no longer wants to go to class.

As a teacher, it is your role to assist the student in making an informal or a formal complaint in order to end the harassment. Look to your school's policy on sexual harassment and follow the reporting procedures.

As a teacher, you are required to protect all students from any form of verbal or physical peer-to-peer sexual harassment. It is necessary to use the school discipline policy as the framework. The student should be instructed to file a written complaint. This chapter contains samples of letters that a school district might use. Next, you should submit a dated, written report to the principal. You also should keep a copy of this report.

As a Building Principal or Administrator

Unlike cases of sexual abuse, in a case of sexual harassment within the school building, the building principal might be the district's choice to supervise it. The liaison can be a dean, guidance counselor, or teacher. However, the superintendent or another central office designee should be immediately informed of any complaint.

- Each school building in the district should have its own liaison trained to handle complaints of sexual harassment.
- To handle harassment complaints, we recommend using a team made up of both male and female members. This makes it easier for the male and female students to discuss the harassment, which is typically gender based.
- A school policy on peer sexual harassment needs to be clearly displayed and a copy given to all students as they begin each school year. Policies should be written in appropriate language for elementary, middle, and high school students.

If a teacher comes to you and states that he or she suspects that a student is being harassed by either a student or an adult staff member, you must begin an investigation immediately.

As a building principal or administrator, you should follow the procedures outlined in your school policy on illegal acts because sexual harassment falls under that category. If your school policy does not outline steps for reporting suspected violations of school policy, review with your superintendent what should be recommended to change the existing policy.

- No one should break the confidentiality of any student who reports a suspected case of peer sexual harassment.
- Document all information pertinent to the allegation.

As a Superintendent

Whether a student or a staff member reports an alleged violation of another student, the investigation process should begin immediately. It is also the responsibility of the superintendent to make the discipline policy clear and available in a school handbook and to include in that same handbook the consequences for violations of the code.

Procedures for Investigating
Sexual Harassment Complaints

A school district may wish to consider developing both informal and formal investigation procedures.

Informal Procedures

Informal procedures may be used as an intervention strategy to stop the harassing behavior of one student toward another student. A school district may prefer to follow informal procedures as an initial action because it is generally less costly than formal proceedings and litigation.

Formal Procedures

Formal procedures may be used by the complainant whether or not informal procedures have begun. A formal procedure ensures that a fair hearing will be conducted and that the due process rights of each party will be protected. The purpose of following a formal complaint procedure is threefold:

1. To determine whether or not sexual harassment has occurred
2. To determine the culpability of the alleged offender(s)
3. To determine appropriate actions or remedies to be taken

AS A SUPERINTENDENT

1. Conduct investigations diligently and in a professional manner, or hire a trained objective professional to do so.
2. If an investigation confirms the allegation, notify student and parent(s) or guardian(s) promptly.
3. Document and date all letter(s) sent to student(s) and parent(s).
4. Enforce the harassment policy.
5. Publicize the discipline policy for harassment and highlight steps for reporting.
6. Use the school media to show how school discipline policies are used.
7. Periodically survey the school building to ensure that fear of reporting is not undermining the discipline code.
8. Offer feedback to parent(s) and student(s) on how the investigation process is handled.
9. Provide workshops for student(s) who are frequent offenders of the school policy on sexual harassment.

When a complaint of sexual harassment is made, the superintendent should

- Act promptly
- Take all allegations seriously
- Stress confidentiality to both staff and students
- Document all information about reported cases
- Ask teacher(s) and student(s) to read their statements and make any corrections and additions
- Have each person sign the document after reading it

Commonly Asked Questions

1. What are some examples of physical harassment? Students who report being pinched or patted on the buttocks, grabbed around the waist, or brushed up against are being physically harassed.

2. What are some examples of verbal harassment? Students who are called names of a sexual nature or who are the recipients of sexual innuendoes, rumors, or jokes are being verbally harassed.

3. Are there any other types of behavior that may be classified as harassment? Asking questions or making comments about a student's sexual activities, sounds that are sexually suggestive, stalking a student for attention or a date, and facial expressions that are leering are other examples of behaviors that are unacceptable.

4. What if the intention of the student(s) was not to harass? The harasser's intention is irrelevant. Steps need to be taken to educate the offender about sexual harassment.

5. What should school officials do when a sexual harassment complaint is made? When a case of sexual harassment is alleged (and the district knows about it), immediate and appropriate corrective action should be taken.

6. What is the role of the school board in cases of peer-to-peer harassment? The role of the school board, consistent with local, state, and federal law, should be to openly condemn all unwelcome sexual behaviors in the forms of physical or verbal abuse that have the effect of intimidating or threatening a student. The board should prohibit any retaliatory behavior against students who make a complaint or any witnesses who may be called to give information about the complaint. The board should adopt a written policy to provide evidence and direction to the entire school community about the issue of sexual harassment in schools.

7. What should a student do who thinks he or she or another student is being harassed by a peer or staff member? If a student thinks that he or she has been subjected to sexual harassment by a peer, the alleged inappropriate behavior should be reported *immediately* to a school official.

If a student has been witness to or suspects an incident of sexual harassment, the alleged occurrence also should be reported immediately to a school official.

8. How do you develop a plan for investigation? The superintendent should lead a committee that will define, develop, and implement specific procedures that include

   a. Reporting incidents
   b. Investigating incidents
   c. Developing remedial action
   d. Recording actions taken
   e. Providing counseling to both victim and offender
   f. Following up alleged complaints to evaluate if all procedures were followed

Empowering Students

Educators can empower students by giving them encouragement and support to take action and respond to an offender in school. One way to empower a student is to help him or her write a sexual harassment complaint letter to the offender. Both the target and the offender need to know that the school takes sexual harassment seriously; a letter written by the target should be filed without any repercussion. In cases of extreme harassment, however, letter writing may not be the best response.

At the elementary level, it is suggested that teachers support a student by helping him or her write a letter to the harasser (see Sample Letter From Elementary School Student to Harasser on page 40) followed by a conversation with the students involved. The teacher can bring students together using a conflict resolution approach. The goals for both student and teacher are to

   • *Empower* students to identify behaviors that are uncomfortable and unwanted
   • *Train* students to verbalize what feels bad
   • Have students *learn to listen* to what the other student is saying
   • Encourage children to *speak* for themselves and not "tattle" to the teacher
   • Work with the harasser to *change* his or her behavior

Sample Letter From
Elementary School Student to Harasser

Date:

To: (name of harasser)

I am writing to you about (what happened or what you said
to me)

_____

_____

_____

_____

This happened (when, where, time)

_____

_____

_____

_____

When you said or did this, I felt (describe your feelings to
indicate whether you were embarrassed, angry, etc.)

_____

_____

_____

_____

You must stop this behavior because it is hurtful to me and
against our school policy on student conduct. If you do not
stop treating me with disrespect, I will report your behavior
to our teacher and/or principal.

Signed (Full name) _____

Adapted from No Big Deal, Jr. (1994). *A Sexual Harassment Training Manual for Elementary Students*. Des Moines: Iowa Department of Education.

PROCEDURE FOR DELIVERING LETTER

There are several ways the letter can be delivered to the harasser. Regardless of the manner in which it is delivered, the seriousness of the complaint needs to be emphasized so that there is no retaliation by students toward the person filing the complaint. A major reason why students do not report sexual harassment is that students often make fun of or humiliate students who do speak out. It can be a double-edged sword for students; they suffer if they don't report as well as if they do. Yet we want students to learn to intervene and respond to what happens to them.

One alternative is to have the staff member who helped the student write the letter keep a copy and give a copy to the student who wrote the letter and then personally deliver the letter to the harasser. A second suggestion is to ask a guidance counselor to deliver the letter. The person who delivers the letter can wait while the student reads it and explain that this is a very serious matter, but that if the behavior described in the letter stops, then no further action will be taken.

GUIDELINES FOR WRITING LETTER FROM HARASSER

The harasser writes a letter in response (see Sample Letter of Apology on page 42). The teacher can then help the student (harasser) respond verbally or in writing and offer an apology. The aim of the teacher working with the student is to help the harasser understand and verbalize what he or she did or said that was hurtful and be able to say why it would feel bad if a friend said or did that to him or her.

If the offender, after writing a letter of apology, continues to harass the student who complained, stronger measures may be needed. The next step is for the principal to send a letter of warning to the offender (see Sample Letter of Warning to Elementary Student From Principal, page 43.)

Sample Letter of Apology

Date:

To (harassed):

Acknowledge the letter:
 (Explain your understanding of why the person wrote the
 letter. If you disagree with what was written, explain why.)

_____

_____

_____

_____

Take responsibility:
 (Write what you apologize for.)

_____

_____

_____

_____

Make a promise to change your behavior:
 (Write what you will stop doing.)

_____

_____

_____

_____

Signed, (Full student name) _____

**Sample Letter of Warning
to Elementary Student From Principal**

Date

Student Name
Student Address

Dear Student,

This letter is a warning for your sexually inappropriate

behavior. On (date) it was alleged that you (specify behavior).

This behavior is unacceptable in our school. In our district,

sexual harassment is defined as (use definition).

Your behavior is expected to improve. This is an opportunity

for you to show respect for your peers.

Signed,
(Principal)

SUGGESTIONS FOR STUDENTS ON HOW TO CHANGE
INAPPROPRIATE BEHAVIOR

Each school district can have students generate their own lists. For example, students can make a "personal behavior contract":

- I will smile and say hi to a classmate to whom I was previously rude.
- I will stop any "name-calling."
- If there is a group of kids at school that I previously targeted with unfair behavior, I will try to find out more about them.
- I will show respect for my peers.
- I will treat others with the same respect that I expect to receive.
- I will not condone the inappropriate behavior of other students or staff.

Guidelines for Writing a Complaint Report: Secondary Level

Students at the secondary level should document all complaints in writing. Following are a suggested outline for documenting a sexual harassment incident and sample letters for use with secondary students.

Sample Complaint Report

Date:

What happened:

When it happened:

Where it happened:

Who harassed:

Witness(es), if any:

What harasser said or did:

What I said or did:

How I felt:

How harasser responded:

Quotes:

**Sample Letter From
Secondary Student to Peer Harasser**

Date:

To: (name of harasser)

You have been saying things to me such as (use quotes) about me (my breasts or other remarks) that make me feel (angry, violated, uncomfortable). These comments (or physical touching) are against our school policy on how to behave. I have told you (number of times) that I don't like it when you (say comments and/or touch me) act inappropriately. Stop this behavior or the school will bring action against you for sexually harassing me. There are at least two other students who have witnessed your behavior and have agreed to come forward if necessary. No further disciplinary action will be taken if you stop this inappropriate behavior.

Signed
(Student name)

cc: Principal
    Guidance counselor
    Other designated mediators

Sample Letter to Secondary Student From Principal About Inappropriate Behavior: Peer-to-Peer Harassment

Date

Student Name
Student Address

Dear (Name):

This letter is to advise you about a complaint I received about your inappropriate behavior in (lunchroom, class, gym, or other place in school). The complaint states that on (date) you said/did (name of inappropriate behavior). This behavior is unacceptable and violates the school's policy on conduct (and/or sexual harassment policy).

Our school policy states: (use definition from school handbook or other to define what constitutes a violation of the school code on conduct).

You are assigned the following date(s) to meet with (designated person) to discuss how you will improve your conduct. If you do not fulfill this obligation and improve your behavior, you will be subject to disciplinary action (as outlined in our school handbook).

Sincerely,
(Principal)

cc: Student file
Complainant file

GUIDELINES FOR ADULT INTERVENTION

- Help harassed write letter to student
- Mediate between students
- Handle cases individually
- Treat all students with respect
- Train peer mediators/student advocates

Policy and Parents

Some districts prefer to think about investigations with a prevention approach. Arrange workshops for parents in which a healthy environment is outlined and offer parents the following three options for dealing with children in the event of sexual abuse.

1. Notify me before you speak to my child—I wish to be present.
2. Notify me before you speak to my child—so we can determine the best course of action.
3. Notify me that my child is being questioned.

Policies: Building a Prevention Program

Building a prevention program in your school that will create a safer and healthier environment for the entire school includes several components. These consist of surveying the school, teaching about policies, training the staff, and creating a bill of rights. Some steps may overlap, whereas other aspects of the program will be ongoing.

SURVEYING YOUR SCHOOL

A survey of your school is necessary to assess the types of harassing or abusive behaviors that typically go unreported. Such a survey will also reveal gaps in student, teacher, or administrator knowledge of harassment or abuse.

The school survey should include everyone. The method of the survey can be written or verbal, but it should include an anonymous questionnaire. This allows an opportunity for individuals in the school environment to address anonymously concerns they may not feel comfortable raising in a public forum. Any student or employee leaving or transferring from the school should be surveyed to determine whether sexual harassment was a factor in the decision to leave.

The student survey should elicit narratives of behaviors that they may not have learned to code as sexual harassment. An example might be a boy who is continually picked on in class as the jock of the school. The teacher and other students joke about him having enough brains to go with his muscles. If you were simply to ask this student if he experiences sexual harassment in any of his classes, his answer might very well be no. A better question would be, *Does anything happen in any of your classes that makes you feel like you are the target of a certain type of behavior because of your sex or appearance?* With this question, the student would be more likely to comment about the situation in class, even though he has not been able to define it as sexual harassment. This is the type of information you will need to gather for your survey, because often it is the subtle forms of harassment that contribute to and build up into a larger harassing environment.

Sample Questions for Student Surveys

- Does anything happen in any of your classes that makes you feel you are the target of a certain type of behavior because of your sex or appearance?
- What type of joking by friends and/or teachers makes you feel uncomfortable?
- Do boys or girls comment about your physical appearance (e.g., hair, breast size, muscles, buttocks)?
- Have you ever been touched inappropriately? When and how did this happen?

These types of questions do not explicitly ask if a student is being sexually harassed and how, but serve to better understand the behaviors that often are not coded as sexual harassment. One of the most difficult tasks for students and adults is learning how to determine if something is sexual harassment.

The survey for adults and staff should follow a similar format. The questions asked in that survey also should enable the adults and staff to discuss behavior that they have not yet coded as sexual harassment. A perfect example is the standard comment made all too often by teachers when a boy teases or hits on a girl: "Don't pay him any attention, he's only doing it because he likes you." Such behavior is a form of sexual harassment, and the questions you pose on your survey could help uncover this type of behavior.

The methods used to survey staff and students should be consistent. All surveys should be distributed at the same time to all students, all staff, or the entire school. Individuals should have an opportunity to complete the survey in a confidential manner.

Possibilities for distribution include homeroom, gym periods, and mailboxes. There could be a central drop-off in the main office for all completed surveys that are placed in a sealed envelope and coded as staff or student. The way in which you decide to implement your program will vary from school to school. The most important considerations to keep in mind are confidentiality and seriousness.

FORM A SEXUAL HARASSMENT/ABUSE COMMITTEE

As with most school agendas, a committee should be selected to focus on the needs of the district and then draft a policy. The members of the committee should represent different groups in the school organization, including teachers, administrators, parents, social workers, noninstructional staff, and students.

One way to draft policy is through the use of focus groups. A focus group can be used to define sexual abuse as it is perceived by the community and as it is defined in federal, state, and local laws. Focus groups can provide information and offer guidelines about the nature of sexual harassment and abuse in schools. Members of the school community can be placed into focus groups based on their area of interest.

Teacher and Administrator Focus Groups. These groups often define the administration's role during an investigation, the teacher's role, the union's role, and perceptions of problems in schools. These groups are likely to discuss what is appropriate behavior for school personnel and the dilemma for educators of wanting to be positive with students, yet being afraid to touch them. Other possible topics might include how to promote a healthy atmosphere in schools and how to avoid allegations of sexual abuse. The procedures for handling investigations, the means for documentation, and who to consult might also be determined.

Student Focus Groups. These groups are likely to discuss what is or is not appropriate behavior, what behaviors make them feel uncomfortable, and how to write a report. Student groups can also highlight appropriate and effective ways to communicate with each other.

The key communicator should regroup the discussants from both groups for further meetings on policy writing and the dissemination of information about child sexual abuse or sexual harassment by staff members.

TEACHING ABOUT POLICIES

Dealing with issues of sexual harassment in your school is a continuation of the educational process. It involves teaching and re-education. But first you need to create a policy.

This can be done by a committee using input from the school community. The school surveys will be reviewed and discussed by the committee and community to create a districtwide policy on sexual harassment. After the policy is in place, the work of creating an environment that adheres to the policy begins.

Policies on sexual harassment and sexual abuse should include nonsexist language and state the expectations for the school environment. They also should include a statement of what will not be tolerated in the environment.

Educating individuals in your school about sexual harassment and sexual abuse must be done under conditions that are nonthreatening and that promote discussion. Sexual harassment and abuse prevention are educational issues that should pervade all areas of the curriculum, and every opportunity should be taken to include them. Examples include

- Inviting guest speakers to address the issues
- Displaying posters around the school
- Adding the topics to health education curriculum
- Discussing and working to eliminate sexism in all curriculum materials

Initially, your school might consider providing a weekend retreat for students with a focus on dealing with sexual harassment and finding more positive ways to interact with each other. Lessons that are devoted to understanding and dealing with sexual harassment should be included all classes.

Provide ongoing training for staff members in workshops and seminars. The district also might consider holding special training sessions for school personnel such as bus drivers, gym teachers, cafeteria workers, and secretarial staff.

SUGGESTIONS FOR POLICIES

- Use clear and simple language
- Educate the students and staff as to the definitions of sexual harassment and sexual abuse
- When drafting policy, include teachers, administrators, students, parents, school attorneys, and school board
- Make students and staff aware of the policy, and review it at least annually for *new* students and staff
- Print a brochure, to be available at all times, that states the policy and clearly explains how to make a complaint

There are myriad ways to incorporate the education of the sexual harassment or sexual abuse policy into the curriculum. Most important is that it is implemented and that it pervades all aspects of schooling. It should not be treated as an aside or a one-time training event. The issue must remain in the forefront of your school policy and eventually it will become a natural part of the school environment.

An example of a model sexual harassment policy follows.

Model School Policy on Comprehensive Harassment*

I. The Policy
  A. It is the policy of the _____ Community
     Schools to maintain a learning and working environment
     that is free from harassment. No employee or student of
     the district shall be subjected to sexual harassment nor
     shall any employee or student of the district be subject
     to harassment on the basis of race, color, creed, religion,
     national origin, gender, age, disability, marital status,
     or sexual orientation.

  B. It shall be a violation of this policy for any member of the
     _____ Community Schools staff to harass
     another staff member or student through conduct of a
     sexual nature or conduct designed to reduce the dignity
     of that individual with respect to race, color, creed, relig-
     ion, national origin, gender, age, disability, marital status,
     or sexual orientation. It shall also be a violation of this
     policy for students to harass other students or staff
     through conduct of a sexual nature or conduct designed
     to reduce the dignity of that individual with respect to
     race, color, creed, religion, national origin, gender, age,
     disability, marital status, or sexual orientation.
  C. Each administrator shall be responsible for promoting
     understanding and acceptance of, and ensuring compli-
     ance with, state and federal laws and board policy and
     procedures governing harassment within his or her
     school or office.
  D. Violations of this policy or procedure will be cause for
     disciplinary action up to and including expulsion or
     dismissal.

II. Definitions
  A. Sexual harassment means unwelcome sexual advances,
     requests for sexual favors, and other verbal or physical
     conduct of a sexual nature when
     1. Submission to such conduct is made either explicitly
        or implicitly a term or a condition of a person's em-
        ployment or advancement or of a student's participa-
        tion in school programs or activities

(continued)

    2. Submission to or rejection of such conduct by an employee or student is used as the basis for decisions affecting the employee or student

    3. Such conduct has the purpose or effect of unreasonably interfering with an employee's or student's performance or creating an intimidating or hostile working or learning environment

    4. Sexual harassment, as set forth in Section II-A, may include, but is not limited to, the following:
- Verbal or written harassment or abuse
- Pressure for sexual activity
- Repeated remarks to a person with sexual or demeaning implications
- Unwelcome touching
- Suggesting or demanding sexual involvement, accompanied by implied or explicit threats concerning one's grades, job, and so on

B. Harassment on the basis of race, color, creed, religion, national origin, gender, age, disability, marital status, or sexual orientation means conduct of a verbal or physical nature that is designed to embarrass, harry, distress, agitate, disturb, or trouble people when

    1. Submission to such conduct is made either explicitly or implicitly a term or condition of a person's employment or advancement or of a student's participation in school programs or activities

    2. Submission to or rejection of such conduct by an employee or student is used as the basis for decisions affecting the employee or student

    3. Such conduct has the purpose or effect of unreasonably interfering with an employee's or student's performance or creating an intimidating or hostile working or learning environment

    4. Harassment, as set forth in Section II-B, may include, but is not limited to, the following:
- Verbal, physical, or written harassment or abuse
- Repeated remarks of a demeaning nature
- Implied or explicit threats concerning one's grades, job, and so on
- Demeaning jokes, stories, or activities directed at a student or employee

(continued)

III. Procedure

Staff and/or students who feel they have been harassed or who feel they have witnessed incidents of harassment are encouraged to contact the Equity Coordinator or any other staff member. Employees and students are advised that all reports will be kept as confidential as possible and that retaliation will not be tolerated.

IV. Notification

Notice of this policy will be circulated to all schools and departments of the _____ Public Schools and incorporated into parent, teacher, and student handbooks. Training sessions on this policy and the prevention of sexual harassment shall be held for teachers and students in all schools on an annual basis.

Name _____ Phone _____
    (Equity Coordinator)

Name _____ Phone _____
    (Alternate contact)

*Note: The language in Section I, subsections A and B must include race, color, creed, religion, national origin, gender, age, disability, and marital status because these are classes protected by law. Any other additions or deletions are at the discretion of the district. Also, districts may wish to add additional language to Section III. Be sure to include language concerning "any staff member" as well as "confidentiality and retaliation." School districts are advised to seek the advice of their attorney before adopting *any* harassment policy.

SOURCE: Wheeler, 1994. Reprinted with the permission of the Iowa Department of Education.

3

Preventing Sexual Harassment and Abuse

Part 1: Building a Safe Environment

Schools must assume the increasingly important role of providing an environment and instruction that promote healthy physical, mental, social, and sexual health for students. Peer sexual harassment constitutes a persistent and growing problem in elementary and secondary schools, where it ranges from jokes and games to sexual humor, innuendoes, and physical threats. Girls begin to receive and tolerate unwelcome sexual teasing from their male peers in elementary school, but teachers and parents often do not code such behaviors as inappropriate and sexually harassing. Thus the failure to recognize and address classroom giggles and taunts as unwelcome sexual behavior on the part of boys toward girls sets the stage for tolerance of sexual harassment in secondary and postsecondary education (Bogart, Simmons, Stein, & Tomaszewski, 1992).

Although we may see signs of a positive climate in schools—smiles on the faces of students and staff; a clean building; visible evidences of learning; effective interactions between teachers, principal, staff and students—what we are learning is that sexually harassing behaviors are insidious, even in "good schools." Verbal slurs and physical gestures that are sexual in nature permeate the interactions between peers, often with neither the target nor the harasser understanding the nature of such harmful social interaction. A female target who attempts to stop it will be told things like "Can't you take a compliment?" Too often, however, those who are harassed fear retribution and do not speak up.

Changing a culture requires dialogue and education among all individuals in the school. When schools take a systemic approach that includes staff development and student development, both adults and students can effect change. The focus of this chapter is on creating a positive school climate that respects the dignity, uniqueness, and worth of each individual. It is our contention that at the core of creating a school climate in which respect for each individual is central rests the need to understand not only what constitutes sexual harassment but to understand the roots of sexual harassment. Sexual harassment is a societal issue. It is a human issue, not a female issue. As educational leaders, we must set forth the goal of eradicating sexual harassment in our schools and creating an environment that respects the dignity, individuality, and worth of every person in the school. The challenge in changing a culture from one that is hostile to one that is respectful and caring requires more than inservice training programs and new policies. It requires effective leadership and training, a cohesive staff, active students, and involved parents.

In the following section, we look at assumptions and attitudes about sexual harassment and identify inappropriate and intolerable behaviors that should prompt schools to take action to eliminate. We also include discussions of gender-based inequities as the root of sexual harassment as well as homophobia, another form of sexual harassment prevalent in schools.

The goal of this chapter is to promote a harassment-free school environment. It discusses the training of administrators, teachers, and school staff; promotes effective leadership; and, most importantly, shows how to include students, who are key agents in creating a climate that respects the personal, emotional, spiritual, and physical well-being of one another.

How can we better understand sexual harassment?

ATTITUDES AND ASSUMPTIONS ABOUT SEXUAL HARASSMENT

The danger in maintaining current attitudes and assumptions about sexual harassment is that they serve as a backdrop for enabling sexual harassment to take place. We do not wish to trivialize or dismiss these real concerns but to offer an explanation for why these myths or attitudes are assumptions that need to be challenged.

1. *"It doesn't happen here; we don't have this problem in our school."* Research indicates that four out of five students report having experienced some form of sexual harassment in school (AAUW, 1993, p. 7). Furthermore, we now know that sexual harassment happens to girls and boys in all racial, ethnic, and socioeconomic groups.

2. *"Harassment will stop if a person just ignores it."* The truth is that lack of a response is often seen as approval or encouragement. We know that in most cases when harassment is ignored, it continues and often gets worse, and students can be ongoing targets of harassment for days or months throughout a school year.

3. *"He or she asked for it. Look at the way he or she is dressed."* Sexual harassment is not about hormones or sex. It typically has far more to do with power than with sexual attractiveness or appearance. A particular way of dressing does not give permission to touch or otherwise harass. A "boys will be boys" attitude cannot be allowed to continue. Boys must be held accountable, not excused, for their behaviors and actions.

4. *"Sexual harassment is a way for males and females to express affection and friendship with each other."* Unwanted sexual innuendoes, grabbing, and lewd comments—or even subtle sexual comments—are not expressions of affection or friendship but rather expressions of hostility and disrespect. Truly friendly behavior is not hurtful.

5. *"Harassment is a female issue."* Although girls are the most frequent targets of sexual harassment by boys, significant numbers of boys also report being targets of sexual harassment by boys and sometimes by girls. Harassment is not a "female issue"; it is a societal issue.

6. *"I was just flirting. He or she can't take a compliment."* Not necessarily. What feels like flirting to one individual may feel like unwelcome attention to another. Flirting is flattering. Sexual harassment is insulting, embarrassing, and hurtful. A compliment does not hurt.

7. *"Most teenagers don't intend to harass, they're just teasing."* They may just be teasing, but teasing has become one of the most acceptable ways of hurting or humiliating peers. Harassment is harassment whether it is intended to be teasing or not. It affects the learning climate for students. No one should have to endure with a smile teasing that is hurtful, embarrassing, or humiliating.

8. *"Calling other students names such as whore, bitch, gay, faggot, and dyke is part of peer culture—you gotta get used to it."* Wrong. No one has to get used to name-calling based on gender.

9. *"Harassers are 'bad' boys."* Untrue. The profile of harassers is not specific. Harassers can be boys with good grades, boys who are athletes, and boys who are popular in school.

10. *"He or she doesn't mind. He or she doesn't do anything about it."* Do not mistake a person's not "doing" something as an invitation to say or do what you want.

The school is the prime source for promoting gender equity, which, it is argued here, is core to preventing sexual harassment. When we create a school environment that is free from gender stereotypes, sexism, and sexual harassment, students will be empowered to develop their full academic, personal, and professional potentials.

Part 2: Educating the Whole School Community

Any serious attempt to address the problem of sexual harassment and sexual abuse within a district (and school) needs to involve the whole school community. Strong commitment from administration is essential for real change to occur. A district committee that includes administrators, counselors, students, parents, and support staff can best bring about a common goal designed to end sexual harassment. Within a school, "the principal is central, especially to changes in the culture of the school" (Fullan, 1991, p. 143). The following actions are recommended for a district whose goal is to eradicate sexual harassment, minimize risks of litigation, and promote a safe and healthy school environment.

What can principals and administrators do to build a harassment- and abuse-free environment?

- Conduct cooperative training programs and follow-up workshops on sexual harassment, homophobia, and gender equity/bias awareness and prevention.
- Create and adopt a student-to-student sexual harassment policy. Be sure the policy is in clear, simple language combined with examples where applicable.
- Create and adopt an adult-to-student sexual abuse policy.
- Understand the district sexual harassment policies and recognize and respond appropriately to sexual harassment.
- Understand the district sexual abuse policies and recognize and respond appropriately to all allegations of sexual abuse.
- Know your legal and professional responsibilities.
- Provide clear procedures for reporting and handling an investigation.
- Understand your role with regard to teachers and students. Investigate and take appropriate action if you observe sexual harassment or abuse or are made aware of it. Take a proactive position.
- Learn to respond appropriately to one who is harassed or abused and to be sensitive to behavioral changes in students. (They may be harassed but too afraid to report.)
- Seize teachable moments when an incident occurs in your presence anywhere on school grounds—classroom, hallway, cafeteria, sports and school activities, and so on—as opportunities to raise consciousness about sexual harassment and sexual abuse and to communicate to students that such behavior is intolerable, hurtful, and illegal.

How can we better understand the effects of sexual harassment and abuse on students?

We often may not be aware of the effects of sexual harassment or abuse on students. Recent research tells us that some effects on students include sheer embarrassment, humiliation, uneasiness, fear, an inability to concentrate on studies or work, poor grades, isolation, withdrawal from friendships and school activities, and personality changes. Some of the effects of sexual harassment on girls are feelings of embarrassment, fear, anger, self-consciousness, and loss of self-confidence. Shockingly, many students do not report being sexually harassed because they do not identify or code such behaviors as "sexually harassing" or because they fear retribution. Often, the effects of harassment or abuse result in reduced ability to do work, absenteeism from school, and course or school changes. For instance, the AAUW survey *Hostile Hallways* (1993) indicated that girls reported that they do not want to attend school nor do they want to talk as much in class after experiencing harassment by peers. In addition, according to this study, girls are nearly three times more likely than boys to avoid the person who bothered or harassed them, stay away from particular places in the school or school grounds, or change their seats or stop attending an activity or sport.

How can we build a more positive climate in our school?

- Develop a code of behavior that encourages respect for all individuals and does not tolerate disrespect for students and staff.
- Use gender-inclusive language in all classes and activities.
- Remove graffiti immediately from desks, lockers, and walls. Repaint the walls if necessary.
- Recognize students and staff who serve as positive role models.
- Encourage teachers and students to develop themes for inclusion in the curriculum that promote diversity and acceptance of individuals.
- Include noninstructional staff—bus drivers, custodians, nurses, secretaries, special subject area instructors—in all aspects of planning and training.
- Encourage school groups to role-play scenarios that focus on sexual harassment (e.g., organize a talk-show style panel of students to dialogue about such issues).
- Talk about gender equity and the need for males and females to work together in school and in the workplace.

- Encourage male staff members to be role models for male students by condemning sexist innuendoes, jokes, and humor and by not remaining neutral.
- Publicly condemn sexist activities occurring in school by communicating your disapproval.
- Offer equal numbers of sports to male and female students, with equal access to facilities and resources.
- Develop and deliver a training program designed to promote gender respect.
- Use bulletin boards to provide information to students about sexual harassment or abuse and where students can go to talk to someone in school.

What can teachers do in their classrooms?

Teachers are some of the most influential people in a student's life; teachers need to be positive role models. That means that they must be aware of inappropriate and undesirable behaviors by peers or adults and intervene when necessary. Keep in mind that most harassment occurs in open spaces such as the classroom and hallway and be particularly tuned in to intervene in situations that have become an acceptable part of school culture. Because many sexually abusive relationships are carried out within schools, teachers need to be ready to intervene in these inappropriate situations as well. In addition, teachers can incorporate learning situations and discussions directly into current curriculum.

- Continually educate about issues of sexual harassment and child sexual abuse.
- Use role-playing, film, and literature to facilitate discussion of behaviors that are inappropriate or "out of bounds," including verbal sexual humor and innuendoes as well as physical assault and rape.
- Lead discussions that show why sexual harassment cannot be condoned with the attitude that "boys will be boys," why it must not be ignored, and why it will not be excused with comments such as "Can't you take a joke?" or "I'm just teasing."

- Discuss how sexual harassment differs from flirting.
- Talk about sexual harassment as part of formal and informal curricula.
- Talk about sexual abuse and its progressions.
- Teach children about behaviors that lead to abuse.

CREATE A GENDER-EQUITABLE CLASSROOM

Well-known gender equity researchers define a gender- (sex-) equitable classroom environment as one in which both the overt and the hidden curricula treat boys and girls equitably so that they receive equal benefits from instruction (Lockheed & Klein, 1985). Teachers strive for fairness, yet research indicates that even those committed to gender equity tend to interact differently with the boys and girls in their classrooms. Usually, these disparate interactions are subtle, unintentional, and go unnoticed by teachers and even by students. We now know that these interactions have profound effects on children's self-esteem, academic confidence, and interests as well as their ability to become independent and assertive thinkers. Studies have shown that not only do teachers give more attention to boys, particularly as a discipline strategy, but boys receive better kinds of feedback and up to eight times as much attention as do girls (Sadker, Sadker, & Stulberg, 1993). Most teachers do not consider themselves sexist, yet their teaching practices are often less inclusive of girls.

INCORPORATE GENDER EQUITY INTO EXISTING PRACTICES

Self-assessment. Look at your own teaching practices. Have a colleague observe you in the classroom, or videotape yourself. Become aware by doing a self-assessment to correct gender bias in your classroom.

Examine curriculum materials for gender bias. Evaluate your teaching materials as well. Do the books you assign usually feature male heroes and leaders? Are girls and women portrayed in gender-stereotypical and traditional roles? Do the books use sexist or male-centered language (fireman, policeman, chairman, mankind) instead of gender-neutral terms (firefighter, police officer, chairperson, humankind)? Use girls in examples as scientists, physicians, lawyers, construction workers, geologists, and so on. Teach students to notice sexist language and stereotypes. Examine with students the qualities that girl and boy characters portray. Looking at how you teach and the materials you use begins a process of self-awareness and self-correction of any gender imbalances in your teaching style.

Increase wait time. Studies have shown that teachers typically wait about 1 second for students to answer a question. Not waiting a few seconds longer inadvertently favors boys because boys mostly jump to raise their hands.

Mix boys and girls. In elementary classrooms, students often segregate themselves or are segregated by the teachers. In these classrooms, teachers tend to spend more time on the boys' side of the room or near the boys' tables because boys are generally noisier and more active. Invite students to create their own mixed seating arrangements, or devise a mixed seating plan so that girls and boys are in an environment where they can work with each other, not against each other. Also, avoid organizing classroom activities by dividing boys and girls (e.g., boys-against-girls teams, forming boy-girl lines in hallways).

Actively encourage girls. Make it a point to encourage girls to participate in and lead class projects, especially in math, science, and technology. Cooperative learning is a great vehicle for instilling self-confidence when girls and boys can teach and learn from each other in the group and are given equal opportunity to participate (as long as any one person is not dominating the group).

Notice the quieter students. Because many girls are socialized to be more polite and quiet, they often do not raise their hands or participate unless they are called on. These girls often do well in school and are the kind of students all teachers wish they had more of. The problem is that generally these students are ignored and are the ones teachers rely on to cooperate with other students and to learn more on their own. Recognize and give attention to the students you may be ignoring for their good behavior—usually girls. Recognize and reward students who are following rules and who are not jumping out of their seats for attention.

Encourage all students to ask questions. Help students to feel comfortable with asking questions. By middle school, many girls begin to preface questions with "I know this may sound stupid, but . . ." or "I'm probably wrong, but . . ." Establish an environment where students know and feel that questions are important to learning and that asking questions is actually a very smart thing to do. Point out that "There's really no such thing as a dumb question." Let students know that they are important and help them understand that putting themselves down undermines their importance and the important things they have to say.

Encourage nonsexist student interactions. Encourage girls and boys to work and interact together in the classroom and in school activities in an effort to create friendships that counter the perception of members of the opposite gender as "sexual objects."

Model cooperative learning. Use teaching strategies such as cooperative learning, which encourages girls and boys to interact nonsexually as team players engaged in a common task, as well as cooperation, rather than competition, among girls and boys (adapted from Sadker et al., 1993).

ELIMINATE NAME-CALLING VIA THE CLASSROOM

An exercise for establishing an environment of respect in the classroom requires putting an end to name-calling in the classroom. This exercise involves teachers and students in creating a discipline code.

1. Brainstorm with students some names that they've heard students call each other or that they've been called (if they feel safe to reveal them; most students talk about their "friend.") Write names on board or have students write names.
2. Group names into categories (semantic mapping): racial, ethnic, sexual, class, religious, personal, and other.
3. Ask students to describe what it feels like when they are called names.

4. If possible, ask students to think about how they've responded to situations. For example, girls often laugh if a boy says something like "I'd love for you to sit on my face," but in almost all cases, it's *not* because students think it's funny; laughter is often a cover-up for humiliation and embarrassment. This kind of discussion can help students recognize their own ways of responding verbally through body language and replace their noneffective reactions directly with words.

5. Respond immediately to any violations of student language not directed at a particular individual.

6. Make a schoolwide policy of unacceptable and intolerable language and behaviors in classroom visible.

7. Decide consequences with class for failure to adhere to policy.

8. Support student responses to students as well. (Adapted from Equity Institute, 1988. Permission to use these materials has been granted by Equity Institute, Inc. specifically and exclusively for this one-time use. Any adaptation, alteration, or use beyond this specified use is not authorized.)

EDUCATE AND EMPOWER STUDENTS

Students are integral in creating a positive school climate. For students to change their thinking and behaviors toward each other, they need skills and support. Furthermore, all students need to be seen as part of the school team with teachers and administrators—not just a few student leaders.

- Incorporate the student sexual harassment and sexual abuse policy into the student handbook, or create a separate sexual harassment handbook. Include inappropriate and intolerable behaviors, assumptions and attitudes about sexual harassment, a list that distinguishes between flirting and sexual harassment, and scenarios of sexual harassment. Define sexual abuse and procedures for reporting.

- Provide sexual harassment and abuse training as part of the orientation for new students and for all students at the beginning of the school year.

- Solicit student input for suggestions on making the school environment safer.
- Establish (single-sex) student support groups for people who have been sexually harassed or abused or who are attending classes that are nontraditional for their sex.
- Involve student government and peer leadership groups in creating a school environment that is free of sexual harassment or sexual abuse and is gender fair. Peer influence is most powerful in changing behaviors of students.

DEVELOP OR EXPAND PEER EDUCATION PROGRAMS

Schools that have initiated or expanded their peer leadership program and trained students in basic counseling techniques have greatly helped students talk to each other about questions and incidents of sexual harassment as well as other issues affecting teens. Include students in promoting a harassment-free environment by training them to be peer mediators who are able to recognize situations that need to be reported and work within the system with students. When students feel that they can tell or talk about it, lines of communication open up. Often, students question "Do I have a right to be upset?" or "What's going to happen if I do tell?" Establishing and training a core of peer student trainers on sexual harassment helps build a peer community for students. In addition, peer leaders or mediators are trained to help both students come up with a contract in those situations that can be resolved without administrative intervention.

- Identify student/peer advocate(s) to accompany victims who choose to file formal complaints, and identify student/peer advocates at each grade level as peer support.
- Train high school and middle school students to teach younger students about sexual harassment, sexual abuse, and gender equity.
- Designate a safe place in school where students can gather for peer support.
- Make available the procedure for filing complaints and process the complaints for students.

Six Ways to Help Students
Who Experience Sexual Harassment

1. Help students recognize sexual harassment. Help students understand that they are not to blame and that they have a right to complain and take action.

2. Teach verbal and nonverbal communication. Encourage students to let the harasser know they feel that the behavior is inappropriate. Encourage students to speak up if they are targets of sexual harassment or if they know of other students who are targets. Give examples of how to use body language, tone of voice, and facial expression to deliver the message directly, such as the following:

   • If a person says or does something that makes you feel uncomfortable, say "Stop!"
   • Don't let your silence look like approval.
   • Don't laugh or encourage the harasser.

   Suggested responses:

   • "I feel uncomfortable and embarrassed when you say things about my body. I want you to stop."
   • "I do not appreciate hearing your sexual jokes that put women down. I want you to stop."
   • "Do not put your hands around my waist. I don't like it. I want you to stop."
   • "No, I do not want to go out with you. I am not interested, and I do not want you to ask me again."

3. Write down the specific incident as soon as it happens.
4. Find out if other people have been harassed.
5. Fill out and file a complaint form.
6. Take legal action.

Six Ways to Help Students Who Experience Sexual Abuse

1. Help students recognize signs of sexual abuse. Help students understand that they are not to blame and that they have a right to complain and take action.

2. Teach verbal and nonverbal communication so that students can let the abuser know that they will not participate. Give students examples of how to use body language, tone of voice, and reporting procedures to stop the overtures of sexual abuse.

3. Encourage the students to write down incidents as soon as they happen and make a complaint.

4. Do not expect students to talk openly about the abuse.

5. Remember that the victim is a child who needs support and reassurance that the abuse is over.

6. Take action.

Educating Parents and the Community

Most important for policy and practice is the parents' level of involvement.

- Offer seminars on sexual harassment awareness.
- Offer seminars on sexual abuse awareness.
- Include parents on sexual harassment and sexual abuse committees.
- Write articles for local newspapers and school newsletters outlining what your school or district is doing about sexual harassment and sexual abuse.
- Send home information to parents about sexual harassment policy and procedure.
- Send home information to parents about sexual abuse policy and procedure.
- Involve the PTA or PTO in efforts to prevent sexual harassment and abuse and to promote gender equity.

Addressing Homophobia: Another Form of Sexual Harassment

Homophobia is exhibited in schools on a daily basis, particularly in secondary schools. We recognize homophobia as a form of sexual harassment that needs to be addressed in a school's mission to create a healthy and safe environment for all students. One of the key findings in the AAUW (1993) survey on sexual harassment is that 86% of all students say they would be very upset if they were called gay or lesbian. In fact, for boys, this is "the most disturbing form of unwanted behavior" (p. 23). Males often suffer more from homophobia than do females because of our culture's high expectations of masculinity for males (Sears, 1992). Boys are expected to be hypermasculine and "macho"; thus an attack on masculinity by being called "faggot," "wimp," or "sissy" is one of the most pervasive factors reinforcing traditional male stereotypes. This type of name-calling and denigration often goes on without much attention on the part of educators.

"Homophobia hinders the development of all school children from growing into tolerant and compassionate members of a harmonious and cohesive pluralistic society" (Grayson, 1992, p. 176). It reinforces rigid sex role behavior, and misinformation keeps people ignorant of accurate information and facts. Each time homophobic jokes are told and tolerated by adults in school, hostility and fear permeate the school environment for all students, heterosexual and homosexual alike.

Although teachers may wish to stop harassment and antigay comments, few have had specific training to teach them how to intervene effectively. In fact,

> Many educators remain silent in the face of homophobic harassment of their students, not because they are callous or agree with intolerance, but because they are afraid to speak up. They may fear creating public controversy by appearing too sympathetic to gay/lesbian young people, being accused of being gay or lesbian themselves or even losing their jobs. (Whitlock, 1989, p. 17)

Thus few administrators or teachers intervene when they hear such homophobic name-calling. Nevertheless, educators have a professional and ethical responsibility to foster a safe educational setting for all young people. The following approach is offered as a guide.

CREATE AWARENESS

Mandatory training programs or workshops should be provided for the purpose of disseminating accurate information about sexual orientation and homophobia.

Little exists within the school structure that addresses the unique needs of gay and lesbian youth, and few educators have specific training in working with these groups. Gay and lesbian youth are often treated as though they do not exist, or else they are recognized only as targets of harassment. We must realize that gay and lesbian students are in every classroom. Any adult who works with young people undoubtedly works with young lesbians and gays. An estimated 28% of gay and lesbian youth drop out of high school because of discomfort in the school environment. Not only are physical attacks common against lesbian and gay youth, but verbal abuse is epidemic, and suicide is the leading cause of death among gay and lesbian 13- to 19-year-olds (Gibson, 1989; Herek & Berrill, 1992).

ANALYZE ATTITUDES

Examine stereotypes and the ways in which prejudice manifests itself in our society. For example, with students and staff, generate and discuss a list of names used to refer to individuals and groups of people for the purpose of examining biases and prejudices that people have against others. Look for and understand the parallels between homophobia and other types of prejudice. Examine all aspects of the curriculum for bias in content and materials, and assess classroom and school-related interactions and the treatment of students.

TAKE ACTION

Promote tolerance and respect for differences and individuality. Enforce standards of professional and student conduct. Include homophobia when discussing discrimination, bias, and equity issues. Address negative school-based incidents on the spot: targeted harassment, put-downs (whether or not targeted to individuals), antigay jokes and graffiti, and labeling. Curricula should be reviewed and modified to include information about sexual orientation and to ensure that school libraries and media centers include fiction and nonfiction nonhomophobic presentations of sexual orientation.

Evaluation

Evaluate district efforts after implementing an antiharassment plan. Involve students, school staff, and parents in evaluating results and making recommendations for goals and objectives for the following year.

A SCHOOL BILL OF RIGHTS

Although districts advocate a philosophy consonant with providing a safe learning environment for students, what many students report is that school is not safe. To assure students of their rights and responsibilities, a School Bill of Rights should be established by members of the school community. Beginning with the belief that all individuals have intrinsic worth and that the culture of a school is a major factor in shaping individual attitudes and behaviors, the following is an example of a School Bill of Rights that incorporates the students', staff's, and parents' conception of the environment that students have the right to expect in their schools.

1. We have the right to attend school free of verbal, physical, and sexual harassment or abuse, where education, not survival, is the priority.
2. We have the right to attend schools where we respect and are respected by our peers, teachers, and staff.
3. We have the right to not be hurt, picked on, teased, laughed at, ridiculed, or touched.
4. We have the right to communicate in words what is inappropriate to us without repercussion.
5. We have the right to attend school in an environment that is free from prejudice.
6. We have a right to attend school in an environment that is inclusive of our gender, race, ethnicity, class, sexual orientation, age, language, and physical disability.
7. We have the right to be included in all support programs that exist to help teenagers deal with the difficulties of adolescence.
8. We have the right to be heard by our peers and the school staff. (Based on Bill of Rights for Students in *Project 10 Handbook*, Uribe, 1993)

Summary

The essential concept to internalize when examining strategies used to counter sexual harassment or abuse is that no single strategy (e.g., adopting a policy) will solve the problem. Unless an approach is used that links equipping students and staff with the needed skills and mindsets to changing the culture of the school, it is unlikely that large-scale, overall change will occur. Although advancements have been made in schools, we are still living in a society and working in a school organizational framework that is largely gender inequitable. A comprehensive program that incorporates strategies directed at the whole school community with those intended to change the climate of the school will be most effective for long-term change. Promulgated by effective leadership, a school that is free of sexual harassment or abuse can promote the potentials of all students in a safe, healthy, gender-equitable environment.

We believe that administrators, teachers, students, parents, and the community can create a healthy school environment in the following ways.

Take Action

- Establish a districtwide sexual harassment/abuse committee that includes members of the whole school community.
- Create a peer sexual harassment policy, and develop a sexual abuse policy.
- Include in the district mission the goal to eradicate sexual harassment and abuse and promote gender equity.
- Become aware of attitudes and assumptions about sexual harassment and abuse, and educate to change attitudes and behaviors.
- Identify schoolwide intolerable behaviors.
- Distinguish between flirting and sexual harassment.
- Define behaviors that are sexually abusive.
- Educate the school community on an ongoing basis; challenge gender stereotypes.
- Educate within the classroom in ways that encourage girls and boys to work and interact together in school to create

friendships of respect and to counter the perception of members of the opposite sex as sexual objects.

- Include students! Train them as peer mediators or peer advocates who can train other students.
- Learn and educate about homophobia as a form of sexual harassment.
- Create and enforce a "Student Bill of Rights."
- Educate all staff, students, and parents about policy.
- Communicate school commitment to ending sexual harassment and abuse.
- Expect changes in attitudes and behaviors of students and adults.
- Incorporate sexual harassment and gender equity into the entire school—classroom, hallway, playground, and school activities.
- Demonstrate appropriate behavior.

Strategies

- Include representatives of the whole community: administrators, teachers, students, noninstructional staff, and parents.
- Draw on students for peer advocates and mediators.
- Insist that sexual harassment and abuse be eliminated from school.
- Educate consistently: Holding just one inservice never works.

Further Information

If you would like to ask questions or contribute information about sexual harassment or sexual abuse, contact any of us: Mary Ann Hergenrother, Cooperative Educational Services, 25 Oakview Drive, Trumbull, CT 06611; Yolanda M. Johnson, Laurie S. Mandel, or Janice Sawyer, Hofstra University, School of Education, Department of Administration and Policy Studies, 208 Mason Hall, Hempstead, NY 11550; or Audrey Cohan, Ed.D., Molloy College, 1000 Hempstead Avenue, Rockville Centre, NY 11570.

Resource A: Videotapes

Dreamworlds: Desire/sex/power in rock video

Project of the Center for the Study of Communication. University of Massachusetts at Amherst, Foundation for Media Education, P.O. Box 2008, Amherst, MA 01004-2002. A powerful 1-hour video depicting images from a variety of music videos. The accompanying narration describes the patterns in the images and how they contribute to attitudes about women as easy prey for sexual assault.

In real life: Sexual harassment in schools

(1994). Altschul Video, 1560 Sherman Ave., Suite 100, Evanston, IL 60201, (800) 421-2363. Prepared for secondary students, teachers, staff, and parents. Ages 13 to adult. Educates about the hidden harm of sexual harassment and what can be done about it. 24 minutes.

Is it love or is it gross? Is it sexual harassment?

ETR Associates, P.O. Box 49098, San Jose, CA 95601-1830, (800) 321-4407, ext. 259. Uses an engaging "talk radio" format to present support and advice to male and female teens in junior and senior high schools. 24 minutes.

No laughing matter: High school students and sexual harassment

(1982). Massachusetts Department of Education, Attn: Bureau of Educational Technologies, 1385 Hancock Street, Quincy, MA 02169-5183, (617) 388-3300. Docudrama that presents the stories of three high school women who encounter sexual harassment in school and in the workplace. Strategies for preventing and eliminating sexual harassment are discussed by teachers and administrators. 25 minutes.

Out of bounds: Teenage sexual harassment

(1994). Cornel/MTI Film and Video, 4350 Equity Drive, P.O. Box 2649, Columbus, OH 43216, (800) 777-8100. A video for teenagers that illustrates examples of sexual harassment and effective ways to eliminate it. Also shows how men develop disrespectful attitudes in their teen years.

Sexual harassment: Guidelines for intervention and prevention

(1994). Altshul Video, 1560 Sherman Ave., Suite 100, Evanston, IL 60201, (800) 421-2363. Includes formulating school policy, educating staff and students, investigation procedures.

Sexual harassment: It's hurting people

(1994). Sunburst Communications, 39 Washington Ave., P.O. Box 40, Pleasantville, NY 10570-0040, (800) 431-1934. Alerts high school students to the facts and consequences of peer sexual harassment.

Sexual harassment: The complete guide for administrators

American Association of School Administrators, 1801 N. Moore Street, Arlington, VA 22209, (703) 528-0700.

Sexual harassment: What is it and why should I care?

(1992). Quality Works Environments, Inc., 11835 Roe, Suite 1945, Leawood, KA 66211. Addresses the wide scope of sexual harassment in schools. Appropriate for high school students, teachers, and administrators. 30 minutes.

Sexual harassment: You don't have to take it

Altschul Video, 1560 Sherman Ave., Suite 100, Evanston, IL 60201, (800) 421-2363. Scenarios illustrating sexual harassment and specific strategies to respond. Includes sexual harassment of boys, discussion of rights and responsibilities. 18 minutes.

Sexual harassment in schools

National Education Association and The Learning Channel. NEA Professional Library, Box 509, West Haven, CT 06516, (800) 229-4200. Assists educators and parents in resolving complaints of harassment by using letter writing. Also sets forth a plan of mandatory training for all incoming students.

Still killing us softly: Advertising's image of women

Cambridge Documentary Films, P.O. Box 385, Cambridge, MA 02139, (617) 354-3677, fax (617) 492-7653. Depicts media images of women using examples from ads, magazines, and billboards. 30 minutes.

Teen awareness/sexual harassment: What it is and what to do

(1992). New Dimension Media, Inc., 85803 Lorane Highway, Eugene, OR 97405, (503) 484-7125, Fax (503) 484-5267. A primer on sexual harassment appropriate for secondary students. User guide. 22 minutes.

Touch (video for Grades K-6) and *No easy answers* (curriculum and video for Grades 6-12)

Illusion Theater, 528 Hennepin Avenue, Suite 704, Minneapolis, MN 55403, (612) 339-4944. 30-minute videos deal with sexual abuse prevention.

Resource B: Other Media

The following eight materials are available for free loan to New York State Educators from New York State Occupational Education Equity Center, 6 British America Blvd., Suite G, Latham, NY 12110, (518) 786-3230. Please direct all correspondence to Marni Schlesinger.

Sending the right signals

This video defines sexual harassment and how it can be handled in school and work settings. Three incidents of sexual harassment are shown and then repeated with corrective measures. Has student manual and training guide. 15 minutes.

Sexual harassment: Minimize the risk—3 parts (Educator)

Developed to assist and guide school districts as they deal with issues of sexual harassment and abuse in the school setting. Divided into three segments: Part 1 defines sexual harassment; Part 2 presents guidelines for intake and investigation of a sexual harassment incident; Part 3 tells investigators how to evaluate facts obtained from the investigation, develop recommendations, and discipline employees. Accompanied by leader's guide. 15 minutes.

Sexual harassment: Pay attention—2 parts (Student)

This program has been developed to provide participants with information about what sexual harassment is, what it looks and feels like, how to respond to sexual harassment, what to expect when reporting sexual harassment, how to assess personal behavior, consequences of sexual harassment, and steps to take to support a sexual harassment-free environment. The videos are upbeat, full of music, and student culture. Has supplemental materials. 45 to 60 minutes.

Sexual harassment: What is it and why should I care?

This video training program helps our schools take a giant step toward eradicating sexual harassment. The program addresses all manners of sexual harassment in our schools— student to student and teacher to student, as well as staff and administration interactions. Has guide. 30 minutes.

Sexual harassment in our schools

This program has been developed to provide participants with information about what sexual harassment is, what it looks and feels like, and the steps to take to create a sexual harassment-free environment. It also provides initial information about steps to take when instances of sexual harassment occur and how to identify personal behavior that may be perceived as sexual harassment. Accompanied by a leader's guide. 26 minutes.

Teen awareness/sexual harassment: What it is and what to do

This video is intended for school administrators and teachers for use in the classroom as a primer on sexual harassment. Focusing on student-to-student harassment, this program helps teenagers understand what constitutes sexual harassment and provides ways to address this burgeoning problem. 22 minutes.

Warning: The media may be hazardous to your health

This video exposes the dangers of media models that glamorize violence, fear, and hatred between the sexes. It can be shown to high school-age students to help reduce the problems of racism and sexism in our society. 36 minutes.

Women seen on television

This video blends narration, clips of broadcast footage, and rock music into a fast-paced, critical look at television's stereotypical view of women. Some segments include women as sex objects, the male voice of authority, women as victims of violence, and women being "fixed up." 10 minutes.

Resource C: Organizations

The Bill of Rights Education Project

> Works with teachers to make civil liberties and civil rights relevant to students. Runs summer teacher institutes and teacher/student conferences. Publishes a free triannual newsletter, the *Bill of Rights Network*, available from the Bill of Rights Education Project, 99 Chauncey Street, Suite 310, Boston, MA 02111, (617) 482-3170 ext. 310.

National Coalition of Education Activists (NCEA)

> A quarterly newsletter, *Action for Better Schools*, is available. National Coalition of Education Activists, P.O. Box 679, Rhinebeck, NY 12572, (914) 876-4580.

National Committee for Prevention of Child Abuse (NCPCA)

> A volunteer-based organization dedicated to involving all concerned citizens in actions to prevent child abuse. 332 S. Michigan Avenue, Suite 1600, Chicago, IL 60604, (312) 663-3520.

Rethinking Schools Ltd.

> Publishes a quarterly activist educational journal. Rethinking Schools, 1001 E. Keefe Avenue, Milwaukee, WI 53212, (414) 964-9646.

S.E.S.A.M.E.: Survivors of Educator Sexual Abuse and Misconduct Emerge

A support and informational network speaking out for jus-
tice and change in how schools protect children. The group
was organized for survivors and their families by Mary Ann
Werner, a parent of a survivor. (518) 329-1265.

Resource D:
Annotated Bibliography

Overview of Sexual Harassment

The Commonwealth of Massachusetts safe schools regional workshop: Book I

(1994). Department of Education, 350 Main Street, Malden, MA 02148-5023, (617) 388-3300. Contains overview of recommendations on the support and safety of gay and lesbian students, school harassment policies, and addressing homophobia.

Hostile hallways: The AAUW survey on sexual harassment in America's schools

(1993). AAUW Sales Office, Wellesley College Center for Research on Women, P.O. Box 251, Annapolis Junction, MD 20701-0251, (800) 225-9998, ext. 246. Survey of more than 1,600 public school students in Grades 8 to 11. $11.95.

Project 10 Handbook: Addressing lesbian and gay issues in our schools

Friends of Project 10, Inc., 7850 Melrose Ave., Los Angeles, CA 90046, (213) 651-5200, ext. 244, (818) 577-4553. A resource directory for teachers, guidance counselors, parents, and school-based adolescent care providers.

Secrets in public: Sexual harassment in public (and private) schools

By Nan Stein. (working paper #256). Wellesley College, Center for Research on Women, Publications Department, Wellesley, MA 02181-8259, (617) 283-2500, (617) 283-2510, (617) 283-3645 or 2504 (fax).

Sexual harassment: Building a consensus for change

By Judith Avner. NYS Division for Women, Executive Chamber, 2 World Trade Center, 57th Floor, New York, NY 10047, (212) 419-5842. Final report submitted to Governor Mario M. Cuomo by the Governor's Task Force on Sexual Harassment.

Curriculum Resources

The ABCs of sexual harassment in school: Attitudes, behaviors, and considerations

(1994) by Eric S. Mondschein. Law, Youth & Citizenship Program, New York State Bar Association, One Elk Street, Albany, NY. (518) 463-3200. Training materials developed for the NYS Equity Center.

Establishing school policies on sexual harassment #370

(1992) by Dan Wishnietsky. Phi Delta Kappa, P.O. Box 789, Bloomington, IN 47402, (812) 339-1156. Suggested solutions for academia, legal issues, school boards, and students. $3.00.

Flirting or hurting? A teacher's guide on student-to-student sexual harassment in schools (Grades 6-12)

(1994) by Nan Stein and Lisa Sjostrom. Publications, Wellesley College Center for Research on Women, Wellesley College, 106 Central Street, Wellesley, MA 02181-8259, (617) 283-2500. $19.95, including postage and handling.

It's not fun—It's illegal: The identification and prevention of sexual harassment to teenagers—A curriculum

(1988). Minnesota Department of Education, 522 Capitol Square Building, 550 Cedar Street, St. Paul, MN 55101, (612) 297-2792.

No big deal: A sexual harassment training manual for middle school and high school students

(1994), edited by Molly C. Wheeler. Iowa Department of Education, Grimes State Office Bldg., Des Moines, IA 50319-0146, (515) 281-3848.

Secrets in public: Sexual harassment in our schools

(1993) by Nan Stein, Nancy L. Marshall, and Linda R. Tropp. Center for Research on Women, Publications Dept., Wellesley College, Wellesley, MA 02181-8259, (617) 283-2500. A joint project of the NOW Legal Defense and Education Fund and the Center for Research on Women. Analyzes 2,002 randomly selected surveys from a pool of 4,200 students responding to the survey published in the September 1992 issue of *Seventeen* magazine. Respondents ranged in age from 9 to 19 years. $11.

Sexual harassment and teens: A manual

(1992). Free Spirit Publishing, Inc., 400 First Avenue North, Suite 616, Minneapolis, MN 55401, (612) 338-2068. $17.95, S&H $4.25.

Sexual harassment in our schools: Putting the pieces together

New York State Occupational Education Equity Center, 47 Cornell Road, Latham, NY 12110-1402. (518) 786-3230.

Sexual harassment in our schools: What parents and teachers need to know to spot it and stop it!

(1994) by Robert J. Shoop and Jack W. Hayhow, Jr. Allyn & Bacon, Boston, MA. $19.95. Provides overview of sexual harassment and the broader context of gender issues.

Sexual harassment student orientation: Trainer materials

> (1994), developed by Rosemary Agonito, Ph.D. Cazenovia College Center for Sex Equity, Center for Continuing Education and Occupational Studies, Cazenovia, NY 13035. For more information, contact Virginia Felleman, (315) 655-8419.

Title IX line: Special issue on sexual harassment

> Programs for Educational Opportunity, 1005 School of Education, University of Michigan, Ann Arbor, MI 48109-1259, (313) 763-9910. A 16-page newsletter to help secondary school personnel implement an anti-sexual harassment program. It includes a sample policy, a questionnaire for students, a checklist for educators, theoretical and legal issues, and a bibliography. Free.

Who's hurt and who's liable: Sexual harassment in Massachusetts schools: A curriculum guide for school personnel

> (1986). Massachusetts Dept. of Education, Chapter 622 Project, Instruction & Curriculum Services, 350 Main St., Malden, MA 02148, (617) 388-3300, ext. 285. An 87-page book with legal guidelines, theoretical discussion, intervention strategies, and 2-day and 5-day curriculum outlines useful for teachers or the training of complaint managers. Includes a questionnaire, a series of vignettes and role-plays, and an extensive bibliography. Free.

Resources for Students

Everything you need to know about sexual harassment

> (1992). (Juvenile literature) by Elizabeth Bouchard. Rosen Publishing Group, Inc., 29 East 21st Street, New York, NY 10010. $15.95 plus S&H. (212) 777-3017.

Girls and boys getting along

(1994). Prevention curriculum for elementary students in Grades K to 3 and 4 to 6. Department of Education, 550 Cedar Street, Room 519A, St. Paul, MN 55101, (612) 296-7622. $10 each.

Sexual harassment and teens: A program for positive change

(1992) by Susan Strauss with Pamela Espeland. Free Spirit Publishing, Inc., 400 First Avenue North, Suite 616, Minneapolis, MN 55401, (800) 735-7323. A complete course curriculum in sexual harassment for Grades 7 to 12, with reproducible forms and handouts. $17.95. S&H $4.25. It addresses causes, effects, and laws concerning sexual harassment. It examines school policy and presents case studies. It can be presented in three 1-hour sessions.

Teens and sexual harassment

(1994). Fifteen-page pamphlet. Single copy free. Business and Legal Reports, 39 Academy Street, Madison, CT 06443-1513. (800) 727-5257. Illustrated pamphlet that describes sexual harassment, the effects of sexual harassment, the difference between fun and sexual harassment, and the importance of respect among peers.

Three separate training pamphlets from ETR (Education, Training Research)

(a) *What is sexual harassment?* (b) *Harassment: Don't take it!* (c) *Flirting or harassment?* Single copies free. Bulk prices start at 50 copies for $18.00 from ETR Associates, P.O. Box 49098, San Jose, CA 95601-1830, (800) 321-4407, ext. 259. School imprint also available.

Tune in to your rights: A guide for teenagers about turning off sexual harassment

(1985) by Dr. Percy Bates. Programs for Educational Opportunity, 1005 School of Education, University of Michigan, Ann Arbor, MI 48109, (313) 763-9910, fax (313) 963-1229. Appropriate for classroom use, student support groups, and crisis intervention situations. $3.

Comprehensive Resources for District

Comprehensive training package for a comprehensive approach to sexual harassment

McGrath Systems, Inc., 211 East Victoria Street, Suite B, Santa Barbara, CA 93107, (805) 882-1212, fax (805) 882-1209, (800) 733-1638. Leader's guides and materials in three parts: (a) *Minimize the risk* (three tapes for school administrators, teachers, counselors, and adults); (b) *Pay attention* (two tapes for students in middle school, junior and senior high school, and college); (c) *In our schools* (one tape for community groups and parent organizations). Total cost of training package is $955. The system also comes with a handbook on sexual harassment investigation. Excellent!

Educator's guide to controlling sexual harassment

Thompson Publishing Group, Subscription Service Center, 5132 Tampa West Blvd., Suite B, Tampa, FL 33634-2909, (800) 677-3789. Comprehensive material for staff training, with monthly updates. $287 per year. Excellent!

National Association of State Directors of Teacher Education and Certification (NASDTEC)

An information clearinghouse for educators, accessible only to state directors of certification. The executive director is Dr. Donald Hair, (206) 547-0437.

References and
Suggested Readings

References

American Association of University Women. (1993). *Hostile hallways: The AAUW survey on sexual harassment in America's schools.* Washington, DC: Author.

Berliner, L., & Conte, J. R. (1990). The process of victimization: The victim's perspective. *Child Abuse & Neglect, 14,* 29-40.

Bithell, S. B. (1991). *Educator sexual abuse: A guide for prevention in the schools.* Boise, ID: Tudor House.

Bogart, K., Simmons, S., Stein, N., & Tomaszewski, E. P. (1992). Breaking the silence: Sexual and gender-based harassment in elementary, secondary, and postsecondary education. In S. S. Klein (Ed.), *Sex equity and sexuality in education* (pp. 171-190). Albany: State University of New York Press.

Conte, J. R. (1986). *A look at child sexual abuse.* Chicago, IL: National Committee for Prevention of Child Abuse.

Conte, J. R., & Schuerman, J. R. (1988). The effects of sexual abuse on children: A multidimensional view. In G. E. Wyatt

& G. J. Powell (Eds.), *Lasting effects of child sexual abuse* (pp. 157-170). Newbury Park, CA: Sage.

Doe v. Petaluma City School District, 830 F. Supp. 1560, 1575 (N.D. Cal. 1993).

Equity Institute. (1988). Establishing classroom rules against name-calling. In C. Johnson (Ed.), *Sticks, stones, and stereotypes: Curriculum resource guide* (pp. 47-49). Emeryville, CA: Author.

Federation on Child Abuse and Neglect. (1992). *Legislative issues: Protection of children in school settings.* Albany, NY: Author

Franklin v. Gwinett County School District, 112 S. Ct. at 1037 (1992).

Fullan, M. G. (1991). *The new meaning of educational change.* New York: Teachers College Press.

Gibson, P. (1989). *Gay male and lesbian youth suicide.* Washington, DC: U.S. Department of Health and Human Services.

Graves, B. (1994). When the abuser is an educator. *School Administrator, 51*(9), 8-20.

Grayson, D. (1992). Emerging equity issues related to homosexuality in education. In S. S. Klein (Ed.), *Sex equity and sexuality in education* (pp. 171-189). Albany: State University of New York Press.

Halson, J. (1989). The sexual harassment of young women. In L. Holly (Ed.), *Girls and sexuality: Teaching and learning* (pp. 130-142). Milton Keynes and Philadelphia: Open University Press.

Herek, G. M., & Berrill, K. T. (Eds.). (1992). *Hate crimes: Confronting violence against lesbians and gay men.* Newbury Park, CA: Sage.

Heubert, J. P. (1994, April). *Sexual harassment and racial harassment of public-school students: Federal protections and what state law may add to them.* Paper presented at the annual meeting of the American Educational Research Association, New Orleans.

Lawton, M. (1993, February 10). Sexual harassment of students target of district policies. *Education Week,* pp. 15-16.

Lockheed, M. E., & Klein, S. S. (1985). Sex equity in classroom organization and climate. In S. S. Klein (Ed.), *Handbook for achieving sex equity through education* (pp. 189-217). Baltimore: Johns Hopkins University Press.

McEvoy, A. W. (1990). Child abuse law and school policy. *Education and Urban Society, 22,* 247-257.

Meritor Savings Bank v. Vinson, 477 U.S. 57 (1986).

Natale, J. A. (1993, November). The hidden hurt. *Executive Educator,* pp. 16-20.

National Committee for Prevention of Child Abuse. (1989). *Selected child abuse information and resources directory.* Chicago: Author.

Resnick-Sandler, B., & Paludi, M. A. (1993). *Educator's guide to controlling sexual harassment.* Washington, DC: Thompson.

Sadker, M., Sadker, D., & Stulberg, L. M. (1993, March). Fair and square: Creating a nonsexist classroom. *Instructor,* pp. 44-46, 67-68.

Sears, J. T. (1992). The impact of culture and ideology on the constitution of gender and sexual identities: Developing a critically based sexuality curriculum. In J. T. Sears (Ed.), *Sexuality and the curriculum: The politics and practices of sexuality education* (pp. 139-158). New York: Teachers College Press.

Shakeshaft, C., Barber, E., Hergenrother, M. A., Johnson, Y. M., Mandel, L., & Sawyer, J. (1995). Peer harassment in schools. *Journal for a Just and Caring Education, 1*(1), 31-43.

Stein, N. (1991, November 27). It happens here, too: Sexual harassment in the schools. *Education Week,* p. 25.

Stein, N. (1993). Sexual harassment in the schools. *School Administrator, 50,* 14-16.

Stein, N., Marshall, N. L., & Tropp, L. (1993). *Secrets in public: Sexual harassment in our schools.* Wellesley, MA: Center for Research on Women.

Steinberg, A. (1993). Hallways, lunchrooms, and football games: How schools help create jocks and burnouts. *Harvard Education Letter, 9*(3), pp. 1-5.

Uribe, V. (1993). Homophobia: What it is and who it hurts. In *Project 10 handbook: Addressing lesbian and gay issues in our schools.* Los Angeles: Friends of Project 10, Inc.

Villaume, P. G., & Foley, R. M. (1993). *Teachers at risk: Crisis in the classroom.* Bloomington, MN: Legal Resource Center for Teachers.

Wheeler, M. C. (Ed.). (1994). *No big deal: A sexual harassment training manual for middle school and high school students.* Des Moines: Iowa Department of Education.

Suggested Readings

Adler, J. (1992, October 19). Must boys always be boys? *Newsweek,* p. 77.

Agonito, R. (1994). *Sexual harassment in the schools: A guidebook.* New York: Cazenovia College Center for Sex Equity.

Broderick D. (1993, July 8). School sex shocker. *New York Post,* pp. 1-2.

Brooks-Gunn, J., & Petersen, A. (1982). *Girls at puberty.* New York: Plenum.

Buettner, R. (1995, May 11). Teacher, teen on the run for love. *Newsday,* p. A6.

Burke, C. (1992, June 13). Bronx teacher in sex shocker. *New York Post,* pp. 1, 7.

Clearinghouse on Child Abuse and Neglect Information. (1989). *Child abuse and neglect: A shared community concern.* Washington, DC: U.S. Department of Health and Human Services.

Cohn, A. H. (1983). *An approach to preventing child abuse.* Illinois: National Committee for Prevention of Child Abuse.

Colino, S. (1993, June/July). Fooling around or sexual harassment? *Parenting,* p. 30.

Conte, J. R., & Fogarty, L. A. (1990). Sexual abuse prevention programs for children. *Education and Urban Society, 22*(3), pp. 270-284.

Delgado, R. (1982). Words that wound: A tort action for racial insults, epithets, and name-calling. *Harvard Civil Rights-Civil Liberties Law Review, 17,* 133-181.

Eccles, J., Midgley, C., Wigfield, A., Buchanan, C. M., Reuman, D., Flanagan, C., & MacIver, D. (1993). The impact of stage-environment fit on young adolescents' experiences in schools and families. *American Psychologist, 48*(2), pp. 90-99.

Elder, G. H. (1969). Appearance and education in marriage mobility. *American Sociological Review, 34,* 519-533.

Elwood Public Schools. (1995). *Support staff application.* Green-lawn, NY: Author.

Equal Employment Opportunity Commission. *Policy guidelines on sexual harassment,* Section 1604.11, 29 CFR Chapter XIV, Part 1604.

The Equity Center. (1994). *Sexual harassment in our schools: Putting the pieces together for prevention and response.* Latham: New York State Occupational Education Equity Center.

Farley, L. (1978). *Sexual shakedown: The sexual advances of women on the job.* New York: McGraw-Hill.

Farrell, B. (1993, March 9). Teacher held on sex rap. *Daily News,* p. 16.

Frazier, N., & Sadker, M. (1973). *Sexism in school and society.* New York: Harper & Row.

Hanson, K., & McAuliffe, A. (1994). Gender and violence: Implications for peaceful schools. *The Fourth R (National Association for Mediation in Education), 52*(3), 10-12.

Haugaard, J. J., & Reppucci, N. D. (1988). *The sexual abuse of children: A comprehensive guide to current knowledge and intervention strategies.* San Francisco: Jossey-Bass.

Herbert, M. (1985). What principals should know about child abuse. *Principal, 65*(2), 9-14.

Higginson, N. M. (1993). Addressing sexual harassment in the classroom. *Educational Leadership, 51*(3), 93-96.

Kohr, R., Coldiron, J., Skiffington, E., Masters, J., & Blust, R. (1988). The influence of race, class, and gender on self-esteem for fifth, eighth, and eleventh grade students in Pennsylvania schools. *Journal of Negro Education, 57,* 467-481.

Lanpher, K. (1992, May/June). Reading, 'riting, and 'rassment. *Ms.*, pp. 90-91.

Larkin, J. (1994). *Sexual harassment: High school girls speak out.* Toronto: Second Story.

Lawrence, C. E., & Vachon, M. K. (1994). *How to handle staff misconduct: A step-by-step guide.* Thousand Oaks, CA: Corwin.

McCormick, T. M. (1994). *Creating the nonsexist classroom.* New York: Teachers College Press.

McGrath, M. J. (1994). The psychodynamics of school sexual abuse investigations. *The School Administrator, 51*(9), 28-34.

Mentell, E. J. (1993, November). What to do to stop sexual harassment in school. *Educational Leadership, 51*(3), pp. 96-97.

NEA Sex Education Resolution B-35. (1969, 1993). Washington, DC: NEA Handbook, 1994-1995.

Perlman, S. E. (1991, August 23). Teacher charged with abuse. *Newsday*, p. 30.

Peterson, S., Sarigiani, P., & Kennedy, R. (1991, April). Adolescent depression: Why more girls? *Journal of Youth and Adolescence, 20,* 247-271.

Petrocelli, W., & Repa, K. (1992). *Sexual harassment on the job: What it is and how to stop it.* Berkeley, CA: Nolo.

Pharr, S. (1992). Homophobia as a weapon of sexism. In P. S. Rothenberg (Ed.), *Race, class and gender in the United States: An integrated study* (pp. 431-440). New York: St. Martin's.

Robbin, D. J. (1992). Educating against gender-based violence. *Women's Educational Equity Act Publishing Center Digest,* 1-4.

Rosen, M. D. (1993, September). The big issue: Sexual harassment. *Ladies Home Journal*, pp. 108-118.

Ross, V. J., & Marlowe, J. (1985). *The forbidden apple: Sex in the schools*. Palm Springs, CA: ETC Publications.

Rubenstein, C. (1993, June 10). Fighting sexual harassment in schools. *The New York Times*, C8.

Sadker, M., & Sadker, D. (1986). Sexism in the classroom: From grade school to graduate school. *Phi Delta Kappan, 67*(7), 512-515.

Sadker, M., & Sadker, D. (1994). *Failing at fairness: How America's schools cheat girls*. New York: Macmillan.

Saltzman, A. (1993, December 6). It's not just teasing: Sexual harassment starts young. *U.S. News & World Report*, pp. 73-77.

Seligman, K. (1993, May 30). When teasing turns into sexual harassment. *San Francisco Examiner*, A1.

Shakeshaft, C. (1994). Responding to complaints of sexual abuse. *The School Administrator, 51*(9), 22-27.

Shakeshaft, C., Barber, E., Hergenrother, M. A., Johnson, Y. M., Mandel, L., & Sawyer, J. (1995, April). *Peer sexual harassment and the culture of caring in schools*. Paper presented at the annual meeting of the American Educational Research Association, San Francisco.

Shakeshaft, C., & Cohan, A. (1990, April). *In loco parentis: Sexual abuse of students by staff*. Paper presented at the annual meeting of the American Education Research Association, Boston.

Shakeshaft, C., & Cohan, A. (1995). Sexual abuse of students by school personnel. *Phi Delta Kappan, 76*, 513-520.

Stein, N. (1992, November 4). School harassment—An update. *Education Week*, p. 37.

Stein, N. (1993). It happens here, too: Sexual harassment and child abuse in elementary and secondary schools. In S. K. Biklen & D. Pollard (Eds.), *National Society for the Study of Education Yearbook 1993: Gender and education*. Chicago, IL: University of Chicago Press.

Strauss, S. (1994). *Sexual harassment and teens: A program for positive change*. Minneapolis, MN: Free Spirit.

Sullivan, R. (1990, May 10). Dean is indicted on sex charges in abuse of girl. *The New York Times*, p. 5.

Tower, C. C. (1988). *Secret scars: A guide for survivors of child sexual abuse*. New York: Viking-Penguin.

Whitely, E. (1992, October). Nightmare in our classrooms. *Ladies Home Journal*, pp. 74-83.

Whitlock, K. (1989). *Bridges of respect: Creating support for lesbian and gay youth*. Philadelphia, PA: American Friends Service Committee.

Wishnietsky, D. H. (1991). Reported and unreported teacher-student sexual harassment. *Journal of Educational Research, 84*, 164-169.

Yan, E., & Topping, R. (1993, June 24). School sex abuse. *Newsday*, p. 3.

**CORWIN
PRESS**

The **Corwin Press logo**—a raven striding across an open book—represents the happy union of courage and learning. We are a professional-level publisher of books and journals for K–12 educators, and we are committed to creating and providing resources that embody these qualities. Corwin's motto is "Success for All Learners."